Contents

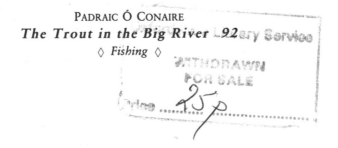

Introduction

STORIES OF IRISH sporting prowess originate far back in folklore. Possibly the earliest reports are those of Cuchulainn and the Red Branch Knights, the household troops of the King of Ulster, part of whose training concentrated on athletic feats. Many centuries later another group of warriors, the Fianna, became just as celebrated – their most famous leader, Finn MacCool, is supposed to have won a game of hurling, single-handed, against a full team.

Hurling, said to be the world's fastest outdoor game, and Gaelic football are Ireland's most popular spectator sports, so it is not surprising that they figure in this collection. Soccer, however, despite recent national team successes has as yet failed to produce even one short story that I could trace. Perhaps one will appear whenever our soccer fever abates. It may be that for the short story, no less than for poetry, emotion is best recollected in tranquillity.

Indeed sport is, overall, a sadly neglected subject by fiction writers everywhere. Is this because they regard it as more suited to the quickfire talents of the sports reporter or because it is considered to have little or no sales appeal for women? Or, could it be that the writer, as a child, had little interest in or feeling for sport, and did not develop any?

The more likely explanation, however, may be that because sport is a game – competitive, yes, but still a game – it does not present the writer with the varieties and degrees of elation that real life can offer or with the dilemmas, traumas and tragedies that are the more challenging and absorbing concerns of fiction. F. Scott Fitzgerald, in his obituary essay on Ring

Lardner, one of the very few great writers of sports short stories, put it thus:

> Imagine life conceived as a business of beautiful muscular organisation – an arising, an effort, a good break, a sweat, a bath, a meal, a love, a sleep – imagine it achieved; then imagine trying to apply that standard to the horribly complicated mess of living, where nothing, even the greatest conceptions and workings and achievements, is else but messy, spotty, tortuous . . .

So for the lover of good writing or for those who seek only to be entertained, sport's organisation of brevity, compression and completeness makes it the perfect battery for the short story's torch. Tension and excitement, drama and melodrama, confrontation and camaraderie, exhilaration and disappointment, pace, plot, humour – this anthology of Irish sporting short stories covers the whole field. Win, lose or draw, the reader will get a result.

David Marcus

Patrick Moran

ALMOST ALL-IRELAND

"WHERE WAS THE Ardagh Chalice found?" the Christian Brother asked. "You, Durkan!"

"It was dug up in a fort in Limerick, Brother."

"How long was it buried there, you, Ruane?"

"It was there for twelve hundred years, Brother."

"Eleven hundred. You should pay attention to what's going on! Why is the Ardagh Chalice so important in Irish culture and history, particularly in relation to the Gaelic Athletic Association, yourself, Nolan?"

Ray Nolan popped up like a jack-in-the-box.

"Brother? Would you repeat the question, Brother?"

"No I won't! Because if I repeated it a hundred times you would still not know the answer. And why, boys? Because when we were learning this in class yesterday, Nolan was down in the Park kicking ball. A real *ball-hopper*, eh, lads? And here's the irony of the fact that he doesn't know the answer: Nolan, so partial to displaying his manly features and athletic prowess at *every* possible opportunity. Come out here, Nolan. Hold out your paw. This will aid your memory. This is the hand that catches the high balls, lads."

Patrick Moran was born in Bohola, Co. Mayo. A returned emigrant from England and Australia, he now lives in Dublin where he founded the Emerging Genius Theatre Company. He has written three plays.

Quickly, from sarcasm to anger, the Brother's face changed and the swish of the leather strap cracked down on the upturned palm of Ray's hand.

'Now, boys, for the benefit of any others of you who may have forgotten, the Ardagh Chalice, originally a sacred vessel for holding the precious blood of Jesus during the Mass, at that time when both bread *and wine* were partaken by the congregation. We can imagine a poor frightened Monk hurriedly burying the sacred Chalice moments before a treasure-hunting Viking cut off his head."

Compassion quickly manifested itself on the Christian man's face and the boys drank deeply of history and religion.

"Yes, how proud we are of our illustrious heritage, and rightly so. That sacred art object, made of beaten silver and gold filigree panels, has become a symbol of Gaelic Ireland. Now, as we said yesterday – are you listening, Nolan – Michael Cusack founded the GAA in Thurles in 1884, and with many other patriots – Dr. Croke, Davitt, Parnell – they rescued our moribund games and pastimes, shook them free from the con-tamination of foreign games and influences; kissed them lovingly to life. And so it was when the Ardagh Chalice was discovered after languishing in Irish soil for eleven hundred years, Gaelic art and culture were, as it were, re-discovered. Ah, the Monks in them days were saintly men. Such faith, such faith. Now, a replica of the Ardagh Chalice was made at the beginning of the century – the most sought after trophy in Irish sport. But when I go to Croke Park on the third Sunday of September and see it presented to the winning team, I see a sacred ecclesiastical art object of the highest order transformed into a sporting symbol of Gaelic Ireland's athletic pinnacle. Our proud tradition. Don't ever forget it, boys. Don't ever let down our proud tradition."

The pain in Ray Nolan's hand was almost gone, miraculously

anaesthetised by this Brother – Oisin, the boys called him – a painter of dreams, a definer of manhood, though he himself had renounced the essential thrust of manhood, a pourer of wild courageous deeds into the eager ears, the wide-eyed, open-mouthed boys of the Tuam CBS, provoking, and at the same time satisfying their eager imagination: a black-cloaked lion-tamer cracking the young animals to fury and taming them with the other hand.

Ray Nolan was one of the hard *shams* who cycled from Dunmore and often walked in the fine weather. He could hear a ball hop at a distance of one mile, the other boys said, and though never a bully, this pleased him. His ears were always pricked up for the sound of activity in the lion's fold of the enemy, St. Jarleth's, when the *Archbishop's Angels* were out practising. Ray's hands were hard. A lash of the leather was no more pain than leaping in the air and bringing down a high one.

It was a different country before television came to Ireland. It was a land of talk and imagination, radio and dreams.

"Bail o Dhia oraimh go leir a chairde, argus cead mile failte go Pairc an Croice. Hello everybody, and welcome to Croke Park for the All-Ireland Football Final between Galway and . . ." Michael O'Hehir the commentator, the voice, the soul of Gaelic Games for so long, introduces *the Match* on Radio Eireann on the third Sunday of September. Mass is over and the dinner is eaten and the neighbours have gathered in to Nolan's house, for not every house has *the wireless*. From Malin Head to Mizen Point, from the Aran Islands to Lambay Island the talking stops. The listening begins.

"BE QUIET!" Mr. Nolan roars, and the very young children run out of doors. The dog dives under the table, well back on the concrete floor, his two eyes reading the mood of the master.

The roaring of the crowd and crackling Radio Eireann try to drown out the voice of the commentator, but Michael O'Hehir defies them and steps up to his top voice register range. ". . . goes up for a high one, fields it beautifully, goes away on a solo run, toe to hand, twice, hops it, is challenged, sidesteps one man, hops, sidesteps a second man . . ." the voice becomes louder and no one has touched the volume control, ". . . there's only the goalkeeper to beat . . ." he is near hysterical by now, ". . . twenty-five yards out, twenty yards, he kicks, IT'S A GOAL! IT'S A GOA . . ." Now the cheering does silence the voice of the commentator and it is some seconds before normal broadcasting can be resumed.

Ray Nolan has his ear glued to the set, his eyes shut tight in an unbearable agony of excitement, as the ball moves again to the danger zone. Time ticking away, the commentator said, and knew that he himself was ticking it away; such power, such awesome power, each second chipped off from the sum total of Time – each second an eternity of anxiety, and the voice could score a goal or not score a goal, and the squirming licence-paying listener could not do a damn thing about it. Oh, Lord, please let this moment end: Oh, Lord, please let this moment go on for ever. Anger, frustration – kick it out, will you – the utter helplessness of the listener to affect the final score, to will the ball into the net of the opposing team – the sinking feeling, oh, they're going to be beat, get it out will ya.

"There is a terrific schemozzle in the square, the ball is on the ground, backs trying to get it out, forwards trying to get it in . . ."

Ray shouts at the disembodied voice, the commentator shouts at Ray. Neither hears the other.

"What are the backs doin'? Why don't they bring on Purcell? Watch the hop. He's lost it. A crowd of old women. That buffer shouldn't be on the team. He has cow-dung behind his ears!"

"Sssshhhh!" says Mr. Nolan.

The word of the commentator is truth. Believed. Trusted. His catchphrases were etched into the consciousness of Gaeldom: time ticking away – a terrific schemozzle in the square – and up they go for it – pretends to go right, goes left – he lifts, bends and strikes – oh, a great save. When the commentator said, What a goal! it was a singular act of heroism for one team and crushing humility for the other.

"... and the sides are level. What a game! What a game! Referee looking at his watch, time ticking away, and I make it on my stopwatch one minute to go ... up the field ... could this be the last kick of the game? It's high, it's dropping, yes, it's over! ... referee blows the final whistle, and Galway have won the All-Ireland Football Final ... and so from Croke Park, se seo Michael O'Hehir a ra, slan agaibh go leir."

And young Ray Nolan dearly wished to be in the middle of the fray.

The young team get togged out. Perpetual motion. An epidemic of contagious excitement. Boys' cackle and laughter, nervous laughter, heads, arms, legs, bobbing and swaying, like maggots unable to keep still for a moment, heads moving in all directions. The Team Spirit. Teamwork. Many is the good man togged out behind the auld oak tree, wind and rain reddening their arses, and later during the game experienced the cow-dung slide, a different cow's-lick from the hair all the way down the back. And each youngster is a County Star, a hero, county colours fluttering in the breeze, on his back a number. As good as two men any day, or three. Now, green and gold, now black and amber, now maroon, now blue, now red and black, red and green, red, lily white, green, white and gold. Fifteen little dreamers with the rainbow wrapped around their shoulders.

Isn't it great to be able to run faster than the wind! Just think, faster-than-the-wind. Fionn MacCumhaill all over! He could hit a ball a mighty skelp and run and catch it before it hit the ground a good Irish mile up the valley. But I bet he couldn't kick a ball from Dunmore to Tuam.

"Come on men," the Captain shouts. "They'll never beat us. Shower of buffers! Smell the cow-dung off them. Come on, let's give it to them. They can't play football and they can't fight. They nothin' but a bunch of dirty rotten cowards. It's a job for the bicycle clips, lads. That poor sham there can't control his yalla scour. You want to tie up the bottoms of his trunks with bicycle clips. Ah, the poor laddeens. Butterflies in the tummy. Run home to mummy. To hell with them, lads. Come on, we have the crowd behind us. Let's give it to them. Come on, men!"

It's nine miles from Dunmore to Tuam and the telegraph poles follow the road, a straight stretch here, there winding narrow bends, through open flat country, and across hilly ground enclosed with over-arching trees. Sometimes the road is traced by dry-stone walling, or earthen grass-covered banks, and in other places by hawthorn hedges. The wires make a stifled buzzing sound like the noise of a wild bees' nest one would step on in a meadow before the bees got out, a sort of angry stifled agitation. But all the same, the humming of the lines is a sort of company for Ray Nolan when he is coming home from school. He gets a lift in the morning, and if he cares to wait can return by the same means.

There are three hundred and fourteen poles between the two towns. Ray has counted them. Often. And about fifty yards between each pole. He knows them as friends marking off time and distance on his journey home; black, silent sentries. And if one looks carefully no two are alike: the knots are in different places and the lie of the grain has the uniqueness of fingerprints. Ray nods to each one, and because of the action of gales and subsidence they appear to tilt back at him. He has an unspoken agreement with them. As a method of getting fit, super fit. Ray walks and sprints between alternate poles.

Here and there a wire is laid off into a house along the road or down a by-road. Some of the poles have only one transverse bar upon which one could crucify a Messiah. Others have two transverse timbers. They are *Metropolitan Crosses,* symbol of Archiepiscopal authority. While others have three cross bars, like the *Papal Cross,* a symbol of Papal authority. Ray found all that information in an encyclopaedia quite by chance and squeezed it into an essay at the end of term exam. The Christian Brothers were very pleased about that and said they would have to tell the Archbishop about it, amid hints of a possible vocation. The other boys sniggered.

Ray would sprint between the *Papal Crosses,* he would walk between the *Metropolitan Crosses* and jog between the *Calvary Crosses.* And thus the journey was shortened, the monotony broken up and the blessing of the old Gaelic poets vindicated – the road rose up to meet him, *go n-eirigh an bothar leat.*

Sweat, sore muscles, pain, tears: push, push, push to the limits of human endurance and when the limit is reached, when all energy is burned up, all manly stamina milked, all strength sapped, knackered, in fact, what a welcome the feel of the cold grass against the face.

"Get up, sham!" A voice from somewhere.

"I'm knackered."

"Get up."

"I can't."

That is the moment when medals are won and lost. Get up and fight on, the mind says. What about the medals? Ray always got up. He became very fit, very strong, very fast. Six-two. And all agreed he would make a fine Guard like his father before him. But his mind, his body and soul were fused and focused on one thing – the sporting cauldron that is Croke Park on the day of the All-Ireland.

The Postman had five letters for Nolan's that day. Mr. Nolan brought them into the kitchen where the family were having lunch.

"I know what *that* one is," Mr. Nolan said. "ESB, they never forget us, God bless them. One for Mary, English stamp. What's this? A brown envelope. For you Ray."

Ray tears it open and reads, his mouth full of food.

"I'm ficked for the founty," he says beaming.

"You're what?" says Mr. Nolan.

"Ray, please don't talk with your mouth full, how often have I told you?" Mrs. Nolan says.

"I'm picked for the County," Ray says and throws the letter up in the air.

"Yer not?" says Mr. Nolan.

"I am. Read it yourself."

"Well done, Ray. Fair play to you," Mr. Nolan says, and slaps him hard on his broad shoulders, as a big cheer goes up from his brothers and sisters.

"We'll make a bleddy TD out of you yet," says Mr. Nolan.

"Oh, Ray, that's super!" says young Mary.

"Oh, I hope he doesn't get hurted," says Mrs. Nolan, and they all collapse into laughter.

"He's picked for the County team, Mother, the first man for five years from this town, and the first man *ever* in our family, and is that all you can say?" says Mary.

"You better write back and tell them you won't accept the honour, just in case you might get hurted, Ray," says John.

"Is she pleased or disappointed, Dad?" Ray asks.

"I don't know, son. I don't know."

But a few weeks later Ray walks into the local with a few mates after a training session. Three ladies are seated in the lounge. As the boys walk past one girl whispers to another, "That's Ray Nolan gone up there. He's playin' for Galway."

"Where? Which one?"

"That one with the brown jacket."

"Oh, is that him. He's lovely."

Two thoughts struck Ray as he ordered the drinks: the maroon flag flutters all over the County and cancels out mere club football. And: Wow! This jersey with the big number on the back, when I pull the maroon jersey over my head, it's a great feeling of pride, yes, but, wow! I didn't think of this before: *responsibility*. Now I represent the whole city and county, men, women and children, the aged and bedridden, and Galway babies not yet born, The Galways in Dublin, London, New York and Moscow. Oh, good God almighty, I represent the Galway souls in Heaven and in Purgatory, and a few in THE OTHER PLACE, the rivers and lowlands, the Twelve Bens, Lough Corrib and the offshore Islands, and damn and blast it, even the goddam sun going down in Galway Bay.

Once upon a time there was a Galway team hurrying to a very important match. They stopped in a certain church to hear early morning Mass. They left before Mass was over. It is said that the priest was angry at this slight and put a curse on Galway teams: a Galway team will never win an All-Ireland, is what he said from the altar. And sure enough the team came back with their tails between their legs, and no team won while the priest lived. And the people whispered in awe at the power of Abel, Abraham, and Melchisedech, to be able to decide the results of football matches from his pulpit. But curses wear thin and spells are broken and thanks be to God, the passage of time and new blood brought Galway back on the glory trail with the elusive three-in-a-row.

It seemed as if the entire County was going up for the match. The big one, the All-Ireland Football Final. The big occasion invariably conjures up the greats from the past: Galway's own Litany of the Sporting Saints. Men like Keenan, Dunne, McDonagh, Geraghty, Leyden, Stockwell, Purcell. You could write a song about them all and sing it sweetly and never get tired of hearing it, recounting their glory on the field of honour. And soon Ray Nolan's name would sit snugly in amongst this pantheon, very much at home.

The Galway team went by train to Dublin in a reserved carriage. The telegraph poles flashed by the window clackity-clack, clackity-clack. Ray sat in a window seat looking out.

"You're very quiet, Ray," the team manager said. "How are the nerves?"

"OK," Ray answered. "Just a tight feeling in the pit of the stomach."

"Good," said the Manager.

Ray did not tell him of the guts and entrails twisted into a tangled bag of banished snakes.

"Galway lads don't need the bicycle clips, eh, Ray?"

"That's for sure."

"Did you see the papers?" the Manager asked.

"No! Don't mention the papers."

"No, no. I didn't see them, but someone said they predict . . ."

"Don't tell me! I don't want to hear. What do they know? Shower of buffers. I don't want to know who is favourite or not. It's not a horse-race we're goin' to. I was trying to keep my mind off it as much as possible. I was counting the telegraph poles along the line. Three flash past the window every two seconds. I've been to Dublin a thousand times before, and this is the first time I've noticed that some of the poles have four cross timbers and some of them have nine or ten."

The poles, leaping over his shoulder, seemed to race back down the line, cowardly, to Galway Station, hurry out the Tuam road and, tiring on the last nine windy miles to Dunmore, slow down to one every ten seconds or so, and utterly exhausted, squat down on the side of a hill in Dunmore town.

"Ray, you're day-dreaming," shouted the Captain. "We have a little game to play."

"I know," said Ray, "come on."

The worst time is the last five minutes waiting in the dressing room to go on. Some of the players make jokes but there is a high note or two of nervousness in their laughter. Some sit quite still. More do a little light training, running on the spot or stretching, but all sooner or later ask about the health of the time: how is the time?

Capacity crowd in Croke Park, green, white and gold flying high, nearby the maroon and the blue. Lush green sward, each blade of grass the same length, manicured to perfection. The founders of the GAA remembered in the names of the stands, Cusack, Hogan, Nally and down in the corner Hill 16. The teams run out onto the field to a mighty roar from the crowd. Ray Nolan makes the fastest sign of the cross in the West. The Artane Boys Band plays the National Anthem. Whistle. Go! Go for gold. For a little gold medal.

*   *   *

Ray Nolan got married in Dunmore, works for the ESB and built his own house. He has a happy home, a loving wife and three children, the eldest, a boy now ten years old who is showing signs of being able to catch and kick a ball. Perhaps it's in the blood.

Ray does not play much sport any more, having reached the thirties, that awful age when the body begins to slow down. He trains the local junior team and promises them that if they try hard enough, well, who knows what they might achieve if they can drag themselves away from the television. He passes on his vast experience. Sports journalists ring him up for comments on important games.

The sitting room of Ray's home is like a trophy shop, one corner of it at least: cups, medals, trophies, plaques, framed photographs, mementoes, souvenirs. The sideboard is cluttered with sporting bric-a-brac, each medal, each cup smiling back, a great day, we won. The whole array is set out in an ordered symmetry, the small cups and medals at the front, the big ones at the back, while on the wall overhead a colour photo of the Galway team in Croke Park takes pride of place with a picture of the Sacred Heart. If a candle was placed at each end of the sideboard, and lit, then the scene would look like a votive altar, a homage to the great Gaelic Gods of Sport who thundered about Ireland long before the GAA was born.

And if this impressive hoard of gold, silver, bronze, marble, chrome, and plastic was buried in a secret place and left there for a thousand years the finder would have treasure beyond his wildest dreams. But, proud as he is of his spoils, Ray Nolan told his wife one day when she was dusting them, that he would give the whole lot for one little All-Ireland medal.

Daniel Corkery

THE LARTYS

SOMETIMES ONE HEARS a great music rising up, up, storming out, thundering; and then emerging from all the overwhelming noise and fury, a quiet heart-easing melody to which one gives oneself up in thankfulness. The gentle theme one thinks of somehow as having been all the time hidden away, kept secure, as in the secret cave of quietness, in the midst of that rising storming whirlwind. Whenever I listen to music built on such a plan, a certain experience, a certain storm-swept night, recurs to my memory; and although the event itself was haphazard, and indeed homely, even quaint, the music, however magnificent in itself it may be, seems the better for the remembrance; for if music teaches us to understand life, life itself teaches us to understand music. This is how the incident rebuilds itself in my memory.

I

No day had ever been so long! Except for the boy, the labouring boy, that is to say, the servant girl, Lizzie, and my old grandfather,

Daniel Corkery was born in Cork in 1878. He was an early influence on Sean O'Faolain and Frank O'Connor. His four collections of short stories established him as one of the leading short story writers of the early twentieth century. He died in 1964.

sitting in the sun beside the gate, giving his face to the warmth, there was no one within miles of us; they had gone westward to the regatta in Youghal. My father, my mother, my two elder brothers, my sister had gone together, all crushed into the trap; and indeed the whole countryside, either by land or water, had made their way thither as well; for that day the Lartys' boat was pulling in the Fishermen's race; and it might happen, we all hoped it would happen, that the cup would once more, after a score of years, be brought to our side of the river. Never before had the whole countryside disappeared like that from their farms and half the harvest still on the ground. But never before had the Lartys entered for the Fishermen's race. How could they, with only a wretched cockleshell of a thing to row in! Besides, they were not fishermen but farmers; a queer sort of farmer, however, for they spent as much of their time on the waves as on the land; and it had been decided, we had heard, that there was no objection to their entering for the race. They now had a boat, a boat of their own, their very own indeed, for they had built it of timber salvaged from the wrecking ocean, built it with their own brains, their own hands, and their own sorry implements.

But the tale stretches back further than that wild morning on which they dragged in the spar of cedar – if cedar it was – from the angry billows, white-crested and loud. That morning all of us, the farmers of Ardaroon, the farmers and their sons, were gathered to the sands to harvest the seaweed from the storm-driven billows. Never before had such a wealth of it been flung into the cove; and this we had expected, for we knew where the wind was facing the evening before and what it would do, as we would say, during the night. That morning, therefore, before the dawn had opened its timid eyes we were there in our sou' westers and oilskins, with long sea-rakes in our hands, already harvesting the ocean. How nervous the horses were, head-tossing, splashes of windy foam snapping at their eyes, their ears full of the sea's roaring! Yet they too, one felt, were entering into the spirit of that strenuous game. When our work was all but finished, we spied, far out, a heavy log adrift upon the waters; but we were too wretched and exhausted to make for it. Anyway we calculated that it must drive westwards, and that in an hour's time it would lie harmless enough in the shelter of Blackball Head. By that time, having finished our sea-dragging and swallowed down the mugs of tea which the women folk would presently bring us from the houses, we would be in better humour for making it our own. After the hasty meal, I helped the others to get the boat afloat, no small task that frightful morning, but I did not sail in her. I know, however, that when they rounded the point they again spied out the log, but it was drifting no longer. The Lartys had hitched it to their cockleshell boat and were towing it into Canty's Cove, the cove they had always made their own of. Old Larty himself was sitting in the stern, smoking his stump of a pipe, smoking hard, not speaking a word; and his four sons – all steadily rowing, for the sea was still angry – were just as silent; they were, perhaps, already making themselves visions of the boat they would build, now that so fine a log of hardwood had dropped into their keeping.

But, as I have said, it is necessary to go back further than that wild morning.

For twenty years crew after crew of easterns, as we were called, had battled against the men of Knockadoon, of Garryvoe, of Cappoquin, of Youghal itself, and never once in all that time had won, so that for long we had ceased to hope of ever seeing that silver cup of victory brought to our side of the river some golden evening amid cheering and huzzahing. The older men used to tell us that the last boat that had done so was a boatful of Phelans − three brothers and two cousins, Phelans also; and the Phelans, like so many others of the old stock, had long since vanished from the countryside. Not since their time had "the one blood", as our saying was, set out in one boat to do battle with the westerns; and only the one blood would ever again do what the Phelans had done, at least that was the people's belief. Now, Larty himself was still a hale man, and his four boys were the toughest in the place, not the tallest by any means nor the bulkiest, but good tidy men, and wild with spirit. Besides, their house up there on the headland, looking out over the sea, south to the skyline and its passing ships, east to Ardmore and beyond it, and westwards to Knockadoon and Capel Island − their house up there on the bald headland, with no other house within shouting distance of it, had kept them very much to themselves; between boys and girls − there were four of each − there was but little difference, and between father and sons none at all.

The house itself, it clung to the headland as by its four paws, there was no corner of it that had not had a buttress flung against it − and stretching out from it west and north was a ramshackle collection of barns, byres, and sheds, built year after year, built anyhow, of pieces of rusty corrugated iron, plates of iron, iron straps and bands, of pieces of wrecked ships, of tarred timbers and polished timbers − flotsam and jetsam of all kinds. In the sheds were their workshops. At night time they set their two "ducks" ablaze − using petrol instead of paraffin − scornful of danger − and so intense the illumination that even far off one caught sight not only of the haphazard windows − large, small, high and low, running along the sheds, but also of cracks and fissures in the walls and roofs.

When, after perhaps weeks of darkness, the people would see once more the bright light striking out into the night, they would shake their heads and say, "The Lartys are at it again," and so saying would go on to speak of the Lartys' farm, how it was going back into heather, and how you might come on half a field of potatoes that somehow had been forgotten or a half-buried harrow consumed almost with rust; while, as for their tillage, in the best field of corn they ever had one could see a crow walking amid the straw. But the Lartys themselves used to make light of such mishaps; what was a half field of potatoes in comparison with a day's racing at Grange, their own horse favourite and one of themselves – Stephen or Michael or Donal – up! Perhaps it was only natural that they should be all of a piece, living so much to themselves in that lonely, wind-swept house on the heights, all of them, girls as well as boys. They laughed, one and all, at their neighbours' concern for crops and cattle.

All through the winter those "ducks" of theirs had been ablaze; we would see the glow of them enlarged in the fogs of evening; and in the dead of night we might open our eyes and find the worksheds still lighted up: looking across the ravine and the marsh, as we had to do, one might imagine the ramshackle house, sheds and all, as floating along in the air, so high up, so terribly alone it was. This time, however, their long spell of industry did seem to have come to something, for here was my own self awaiting news of the conflict in Youghal Harbour. In the cowsheds we were – the girl, the cowboy and myself, when the word at last came to us. Jack Lynch's son had brought it. He rode his bicycle impulsively in among the impatient cows, right through the mire of the yard. His cheeks were crimson and running with sweat; "The Lartys are after doing it!" and then, I remember he turned round crying "Hough, Hough" roughly, for one of the cows was backing slowly, persistently, into him, bike and all. "They had to fight every inch of it with the Knockadooners; and the wind was strong, mind you. They're great men, the Lartys. Sweeney says the boat's a bit stumpy. But she's a good boat all the same – and not a Christian in her except themselves – the one blood!"

How proud I was! The Lartys were cousins of mine – my own name's Larty. Besides, before my people had left that morning for Youghal, I had got a promise from them that when they returned in the evening I might go up to the Lartys for the night. I'd rather a night with them in that crazy den of theirs than a week of regattas. As we sat on the low stools in the shed at the bellies of the cows, ten times over Jack Lynch told us the story of the fierce struggle for the race. He was leaning over the handle-bar of his bicycle, and had his head thrust in at the door. At last we stood up, drove out the cattle, and I made ready to go up to the Lartys.

II

I swept down the hillside on my bicycle, across the bridge at Ardaroon, along the edge of the marsh, and so on to the sands. A terrific wind had set in; riding had become impossible; it was necessary, to my great disgust, to wheel the bicycle along, my head down, making but little progress. Night was falling as I crossed the height between the two coves. Beneath me, coming up from the strand, I heard many angry voices. I made on; and found the Lartys in hot contention, the victorious boat in their midst, as unconscious of their quarrelling as of her own triumph.

On that evening I first began to understand that man differs from man. I had not expected to find them on the windy foam-swept sands of Canty's Cove, still less to find them barking at one another so soon after so glorious an adventure. I think I felt some explanatory thought stirring within me: the Lartys after all were the Lartys! Eight of them were there in a group, Old Larty

himself, his four sons, and three of the daughters. There were a
few neighbours also – an old labouring man who belonged to
the Lartys in the same way as their sheep dog belonged to them;
the boy Mullins, who takes the post across the ferry, and the
pensioned-off teacher who lives in Kenree. Like myself they felt
no call to interfere with the Lartys in this strange confusion of
theirs.

The second son, Stephen, had his hand on the nose of the
boat, and was speeching the rest of them – father, brothers,
sisters. I felt he must have said the same thing over and over
"The finishing touches are not on her. Let none of ye say they
are. She's bright enough now, she's clean and tidy. That wind
will blow a gale. I told ye so this morning. 'Tis overdue two days
and more. I told ye that by the moon. How will it be with her
in the morning after a night of it? She'll be soiled and stupid!
What thing takes the dirt like a new thing? Throw a new saddle
in the mud and who'll clean it ever after?" – here he made a
lurch forward still keeping his grip on the boat however –
"When I'm speaking ye might have the manners to hold your
tongue."

"What am I saying against you?" Michael asked in surprise.

" 'Tisn't you at all; 'tis Diarmuid there."

"Me! Cutting a fill I am."

"Cutting a fill! You haven't the pluck to say out what's in
you."

The father then took up the running: "No, but when I'm
speaking, let ye hold yer whishth! If there's another farmer from
this to the Old Parish could build her – I'm thankful to ye, to
ye all – but she's mine; and ye know it. 'Twas my brain
conceived her. 'Twas I saw her in the dark, every line and every
slip of her. But she's not finished. Don't tell me she is. She's not.
But for all that there she'll stay till the light of morning, or

longer. There are things to be done to her, and I'm dark still on them. But I won't be long so – so I won't."

The wind was rising all the time. He looked about him. He got in the shelter of a rock, and began, he too, to grind up a plug of twist tobacco in his rough hands. In some way I gathered that one party of them were for taking the boat up the cliff side to her cradle that she might be finished once for all, and not left, like so many of their contrivances – a folly, as the people say. The others, tired after their long day of work and excitement, were for leaving her where she was, at least for the one night. "Who's saying she's finished?"

"But what harm will it do her to leave her there for the one night?"

Michael then spoke: he was the youngest, and was somewhat indolent in his ways, more tired, too, it may be, than the others, who were harder: "Sure we know she's not finished; but what's to hinder us giving her a hise up in the morning when we're fresh?"

"You're an infant, Michael," the earnest Stephen spoke again. "By the law of the land you're an infant, and an infant ye'll be for many a long day after it makes a man of ye."

Somewhere was a snigger, but I recall that Stephen himself took no notice of it, had, in his earnestness, no time to take notice of it: "If she lies there this night, and if we stroll down to her in the morning, and who knows but we won't think of doing the like for a month." He did not finish his thought.

Donal, the eldest, was like his mother, rubicund, with soft eyes:

"Say something anyhow. Put an end to it. Up with her or down with her, but anyhow – "

" 'Tis waiting for the dark we are," one of the girls said.

"And a little wind, just a little wind."

By this it was blowing a gale, and nearly all of us had our headgear in the clutch of a hand, right or left.

"Yerra, lave her there, what is she but a bit of a boat?" Of this, too, Stephen took no notice.

"We're the Lartys," he said. "Lift her, boys. Up with her. They say – " with a sweep of his arm encircling half the countryside, "they say 'tisn't in us to finish a thing. But we'll finish this one. Lift her, boys."

From the shelter of the rock the father's voice rolled out, strongly, scornfully:

"Finish her! Finish her! Maybe ye could. But I'd like to see her. There she's there and here she's here," and so saying he struck his forehead with his open hand, "and if she's anywhere else I'd like to be informed of it. Finish her! I'm not against it, but I'm not going to finish myself, after we pulling such a race as was never heard tell of the seven parishes over. Hear them! They're cheering still."

And in the rising wind we certainly fancied we caught the sound of rejoicings coming across the darkening waters from the town. The town itself, nor its lights, we could not see; but we did certainly imagine that shouts and cries and cheering were in the air, caught up and broken in the wilful gusts. But Stephen was not to be turned from his purpose:

"That wind will be a terror; ye know it will. There she'll be in the morning, half-wrecked maybe, filthy and slimy, with sand and weed and dead dog-fish all over her; and speak honest, will any of ye lift her then or bother yer heads about her? Ye'll be saying: 'She's good enough.' And ye won't touch her till the next day's sport in Cappoquin, and on we'll go and we'll win or lose; and it won't matter, for what everybody will be looking out for is what old Sweeney is telling them now in all the bars and snuggeries of Youghal town."

The old man came forward in silence from his rock. His eyes searched our faces:

"What is it he said? What are ye hiding from me? What had Sweeney to say again' her?"

"It don't matter," Stephen tried to put it off. "Lift her, boys."

"But it does matter."

Then Donal blurted out: "He only said what he said ever and always about every boat that ever came from this side."

"But what was it, what was it, my son?"

"He said she's a stump."

We stirred with uneasiness, and we saw that the old man had been dumbfounded. He pulled himself together, however: "Come boys, come boys; we're a bit fresher now. That wind would freshen a corpse. 'Twill be a dirty night, a dirty bad night. Lend a hand, Jack. You too, Donal."

III

Before we knew what we were at we were pushing, tugging, sliding, crushing her over the rough shingle towards the pathway up the cliffs. The wind began to roar; the foam flakes to slash our faces; and the night fell so suddenly that the girls were sent up for some lanterns, for we could hardly any longer see what we were doing. Ships' lamps they brought us. We had got her a little way up and there we rested till the lamps were set alight. They made only a dull glow. I noticed that the moment we took our hands from her the neighbours quietly slipped away; one could not blame them, some of them lived a long way off. I noticed also how all of us had thrown ourselves instinctively into attitudes of rest in nooks and corners where the wind was broken. And I thought if I were finding the work severe, it must have been far heavier on them, for not only had they gone

through the race suffering its strain and excitement, but afterwards had been rowing about the harbour taking, as they
thought, the admiration of the crowds on the shore and in the
boats. Now, perhaps, they were picturing themselves as sailing
that way about and about, up and down, head high, proudly,
in the full view of all, who instead of admiring them might have
been saying: "It's a pity she's a stump." Anyway, the Lartys were
silent now, whatever they were thinking of.

In the glow of the lamps we set to again; and it was slow work
with us. We had a couple of rollers, just a bit of a spruce tree
sawed into lengths, and these we had to be watching and rectify-
ing and shifting from stern to bow; and on the uneven narrow
path they would sometimes slew round obliquely and run the
craft almost over the edge. In places the space was quite
confined; and in the fitful light – the girls shifting or raising or
lowering the lanterns as they thought best – the features of the
pathway would become quite unfamiliar, even to the Lartys
themselves.

"Mind yourself, Donal," we'd hear of a sudden; or, cried out
sharply, "Steve, keep Michael on the inside," or some such
phrase; and little by little each of us sank into himself as we
strained and slipped. Some of us were becoming sullen, and
others irritable in the anxiety; and then, as I have often noticed
about other things – a plough, a motor, a chaff-cutter – the
boat, through dint of handling her, of struggling with her, began
to take on a life of her own. Sometimes we felt her as resisting
us, as being stubborn, going in every direction except where we
wanted; at other times, however, she became, for a spell, quite
tractable; and we all moved on at a little run over a certain
couple of yards of ground. At other times again we could hardly
take a move out of her; we heard her straining, creaking, sliding,
scraping – all this, however, was but the noise of timber, earth

and stone — not somehow the voice of the boat herself; that was hushed up within her; she was a dumb spirit, resisting our desires.

Stephen, naturally, held out best. He spoke but little. Now and then in a drop of the wind he would breathe out huskily: "Up! Up! Up!" and hearing him we would put all the strength of our backs into the work.

Soon the night broke into wild windy rain and we grew still more miserable.

About half-way up was a sort of level known to us as the Quay — a bit of protecting wall once ran along the edge of the cliff in this place — and the thought came to me that in this lobby, as it were, she would do very well for the night; in the morning we could lift her up the rest of the path easily enough. By this it had become a night of utter darkness and of raging fitful winds; below us we heard the waves passionately breaking themselves on the rocks or withdrawing precipitately back from the grasp of the narrow gullies; out on the sea we heard, almost felt, the meeting of wave and wave, but the fall of their crests, the whiteness of their foam, we could not see. And we didn't try. To think of the height we were now on, of the little space we had to manoeuvre in, of the snarling fury about and beneath us — was to feel a coldness gripping one about the back of the head and neck. I began to pray that Stephen would be satisfied with the quay as a resting place, for on Stephen I felt it all depended. But I lost hope entirely when I caught his words in the whistling of wind and rain:

"Hawn — awm — she'd — be — a lovely sight by this down below — " The rest was lost in the bellowing.

Again we dragged at the dead weight of the boat: sometimes now the wind would make a grab at her, getting into the pit of her, and we had just to hold her till the gust had died.

"Up on the quay with her, up, up!"

But just here the path was steepest; and we were all in the worst of humour, yet Stephen was in the midst of us, and not a man took a hand from her till we had got her bow on the edge of the level. "All together," then cried Stephen, and we rushed her along into the middle of the level space. "She's safe as a house," Diarmuid gasped angrily and drew back, flung himself back into the lee of the cliff. Old Murt, the labouring man, rushed also. So with us all, as by a signal. And we all groped to find snags of rock to cling on to. We were muttering too, I can't remember what. And Stephen overheard us:

"Is it leave her there ye would?"

The storm answered him. As for us, we were flat against the face of the cliff, our faces turned from the sea.

"Is it for leaving her there ye are," he roared again at us, his right hand gripping the gunwale of the boat.

We could not have chosen a worse place, for that level space swung round a sort of blunted spit of land, as a gallery might be carried round the outside of the apse of a church – and it was open breasted to the gale.

"Where are ye?" we heard Stephen's voice again, "where are ye?"

"The boat! The boat!" suddenly cried Michael; and – a strange thing – we could have sworn that it was Stephen's voice! And Michael, you'd think, was not a bit like Stephen. Someone swung a lamp, and in the beams we saw our boat stir, lift a shoulder like a porpoise and dive over the edge, slicing it with her keel!

We dared not stir. "Stephen!" someone cried. We were struck with cold, frozen, until we heard Stephen's voice answer: "Here!" and then, "Where are ye?" And the next moment he flung himself in among us as if, by an effort of will, he had dragged himself from the edge that the boat had swooped down from. What most of all unnerved us was that none of us heard the boat crash upon the rocks beneath. That left us with a sense of vast and gaping vacancy out before us and beneath us. The old man roared at us: "Chest − shoulders − 'gainst the cliff − 'gainst the cliff − edge along − edge along − along." By inches then we began to move. The girls caused us no anxiety, they were accustomed to fend for themselves. Indeed it was one of them who still kept one of the lamps by her; the other, we discovered, had been left derelict in a crevice when we began our progress. That progress we now measured by its beams. When we could no longer see them we knew we had got past the danger point. Only the person nearest was visible to one, and even that person was often lost in the thick darkness. A voice would suddenly cry out sharp and tense:

"Michael?" or "Donal, where are you?" or "Nora?" and the voices had to roar to defeat the voices of the winds.

We had not very far to go before we found shelter. Where the path began to rise again it went between two rocks − one had in some ancient day shaled off from the other − and between these rocks we now gathered like scared sheep, drenched, torn, winded, yet safe − which was everything. I saw how anxious the sons were about their father, how they would make some excuse for touching him:

"Turn up your collar."

"If you tied the scarf."

And indeed for that matter we felt like touching one another, like shaking hands foolishly with one another. But after a few moments we were laughing and chaffing about it all; and the old man was babbling over and over: " 'Twouldn't do to have one of us missing, 'twouldn't do at all."

That night! That night in the Lartys' kitchen! When we had

put on dry clothes and swallowed down many cups of tea and eggs and cake, we drew up around the open fire and heard the great race recounted in a hundred ways – what this man and that man had said before the race and what they had to say after it, and how the Cappoquin men had taken their beating, and what the Knockadooners had said, and so on and so on! And all the time the winds were howling around the house, baffled one would think, so many tricks they were trying, to judge by their swoonings and whinings. We would often hear coming from the workshops a dreadful rattle of loosened sheets of iron or bars or planks, and sometimes a crash, when some portion of a shed was stripped off; or in some interval of the pother the wild cry of some foolish calf, groaning, with stretched throat, with anxious eyes – we could picture it – but how little it all disturbed us, this hubbub with its wild crashes – if indeed it did not create in our spirits a warmth altogether beyond the glow of victory. As I have said, whenever I heard gladsome lightly leaping music emerging from great thundering passionate harmonies I think of the crowd of us there around the wide and open hearth, and all the laughing and sport we made, the sense of danger seasoning it. And I remember how it crossed my mind that though my father and brothers were wiser than the Lartys, and better farmers, and richer, they would not have taken the loss of such a serviceable thing as a new boat so lightly as the Lartys were taking it in that crazy house of theirs that the winds might wreck. But this I did not think of until well on in the night – for we had no thought of breaking up the merriment – when the old man with a whirlwind of words and gestures imposed silence on us for a little while. I saw him rise up – I can see him now, his lump of a body square-set, ungainly, against the glowing fire – I saw him gesturing, imploring our attention, calling us by name one after another, stamping out a burst of laughter here, a burst of laughter there, maintaining silence with one hand while with the other he beckoned the girls to join the circle as well as the others, to leave the work they were at undone – whatever it was. And at last when he found himself in control I remember how he began by saying: "Whishth now, let ye whishth, all of ye. Look, 'tis how to-morrow we'll be going to Mass. We'll hear whatever Father Mulcahy will have to say to us. Who knows but he might have something good to say this time. But we'll be going to Mass; and the Heddermans and the Griffins and the Powers and the Barrons, the Frahers, the Walshes, the Motherways – all of them will be gathering about us and making great talk over the race we made, and talking, and talking. Now boys, girls – we'll all be on the one word – the one word for all of us. What will we say to them? Listen now. Ye're the Frahers. Ye're the Powers. Ye're all around me. And I'll say: 'Yes, we made a good fight. We had to make a good fight. The Knockadooners are good ones. Captain Michaleen Barry is good to steer a boat, none better. It gave us all we could do to beat them. But look at what we had! What had we, I ask ye? What had we, I ask ye all? Glory be! a stump of a boat we slapped together in the night time! After our day's work, a thing we slapped together! The sea swept it away from us last night. All the better. What would we be doing with it except running races from Tramore to Crookhaven, like the Phelans of old, rousing the country against us, and maybe neglecting our farm!'"

And he looked at us as he was going to look at the Frahers, the Powers, the Heddermans and the rest of the sensible folk on the morrow. In his eye there was a twinkle, half challenge, half mockery.

Liam O'Flaherty

THE WING THREE-QUARTER

THERE WAS A white frost on the ground. The whole field was covered with it. Here and there the turf had been cut and bruised by the tramping of feet during the practice matches of the past fortnight. And the frost had formed these patches of muddy, torn earth into hard cakes, pointed and sharp. The earth resounded under the feet of the fellows as they rushed out from the pavilion. You could see the fellows' breath rushing from their mouths through the thin, freezing air in shooting columns, like puffs of steam from an engine.

A great cry arose from the crowd on the touchlines as the school team dashed out. All the boys waved their caps in the air and yelled out the school war-cry. It was the final of the schools' cup. "Hurrah! Hurrah! Go on, Blackburn! Good old Fitz! Don't funk it, Regan!"

Regan rushing out with long strides heard this warning and shuddered. He ground his teeth and paced out at his full speed, dashing across the field like lightning to the far goal-post. When they saw him run the whole crowd burst into a wild cheer. God! He was as fast as a hare. If he weren't such a funk . . .

Liam O'Flaherty was born on Inishmore, the largest of the Aran Islands, in 1896. He joined the Irish Guards in 1915 and fought at the Somme. Regarded as a world master of the short story, he also wrote fifteen novels. He died in 1984.

Regan stood by the goal-post stamping his feet and slapping his hands under his armpits waiting for the line-up. He was afraid to look at the crowd or at the white frost on the field. But he was acutely conscious of the crowd and of the frost. He didn't know which he feared most, the frost or the crowd. That dreadful sensation of being hurled down violently on to the ice-hard ground by a huge forward, the dreadful tackle about the knees, the sudden thump of hands clasping him about the knees and hurling his body into the air, the grunt and hot outrush of breath as the fellow clasped him and rolled with him to the earth, and then the louder thud as his own body hit the earth and all his members shook with the savage concussion. The frost and the tackle! Tackled in that frost. It was terrible. But he mustn't funk. If he did all that horrid crowd of boys would yell and boo . . . not only now but afterwards, during the whole term . . . That rotten funk Regan.

He looked splendid in his football outfit. A slim tall fellow with long, sleek, fair hair combed back on his poll and a long, thin nose. But he was too neat and there were thick tape bandages on his knees, which none of the other fellows were wearing. They sort of sneered at him in the pavilion when he was putting them on.

The whistle blew. The captain waved his arm and cried out. Everybody rushed into line. A low murmur passed over the touchlines. Everybody waited. The other side looked very strong. Their forwards looked massive, lurched forward in a line behind their captain who was kicking off. Then there was a dull thud as the ball bounded off, then a roar and the whole field was in motion, rushing, panting and shouting, while on the touchlines the fellows shook rattlers and cheered.

The ball stayed in mid-field and Regan was left out on the right wing without anything to do. He kept running backwards and forwards as the ball advanced into the enemy's territory or switched back again towards his own line. He had positively no interest in the progress of the game and he kept praying all the time that it would not come near him. He was almost stupefied with terror and was only half aware of his surroundings, of the roaring and the rushing of feet. Then suddenly, after ten minutes' play, the enemy's backs got the ball from the scrum.

Regan's heart stopped beating but he rushed forward to mark his man, a short, thick-set fellow, with a curly, dark head and square jaws. He saw the ball pass out rapidly to this man, as the out half and then the centre were tackled and felled. His man got the ball from a long pass, slipped it under his arm, lowered his head and dashed forward. A great cry went up. "Take him, Regan. By the knees. By the knees. Down on him. Down on him."

Thud, thud, thud-thud . . . The other fellow made for the touchline, running at a tremendous pace to get past Regan's flank. Regan flew up to him like lightning and then when he was within tackling distance he gritted his teeth and prepared to stoop for the fellow's knees. But just at that moment his heart failed. Instead of plunging in, he let himself fall limply and his hands just grazed the fellow's back. Regan stumbled forward and fell on his knees and as he arose he could hear a savage yell from the touchline and the cry: "Funk! Ye funked it. After him. Funk!" He jumped to his feet again and sped after his man. The fellow was sprinting straight for the line but the full-back was waiting for him. Regan dashed on and reached his man once more, just as the full-back stooped to tackle him. They both got him and the three of them rolled over and over on the ground. Saved.

But the other fellows looked at him with angry faces and the captain rushed past him muttering something. Regan stood behind the scrum trembling. The contact with the frost-covered field had shaken him and he felt a terrific desire to rush off somewhere and hide. His teeth were chattering. But again he got a respite. The forwards took the ball on their toes and made a tremendous rush with it half-way up the field. For the next quarter of an hour it was again a forward game and Regan was left in peace.

Then a little before half-time Regan got the ball from a scrum. He received the ball at mid-field from a line-up at touch and he had almost the whole width of the field to double past his opponent. The whole crowd raised a tremendous shout and several boys threw their caps in the air, because this was the very opportunity that always enabled Regan to score. His miraculous speed was his only asset, and here was an open field before him. In fact, a crowd broke from the railings on either side and dashed down to the enemy line to see the touch-down.

But Regan could not control his nerves. He dashed off well enough, and doubling in a wide arc, he passed the two centre three-quarters and came face to face with his own man on the wing. Then instead of spurting at his limit and going straight ahead, he ran in a still wider arc, going backwards instead of going forwards. Everybody shouted: "Run straight. Run straight". But Regan could not nerve himself to face his man. He kept doubling out until at last he ran into touch. There was dead silence. The fellows were too broken-hearted even to jeer at him.

Then, a few minutes later, after desultory play among the forwards, the half-time whistle blew. A servant ran on to the field with the lemons. The two teams gathered about their captains and trainers, and putting their heads togther discussed plans. Regan threw himself on the ground and drooped his head. He could hear the babel of voices around him, but he didn't understand what was being said. He felt terribly ashamed and there was a red blur before his eyes. Somebody chucked a lemon towards him, shouting: "Catch". He didn't move to take it. It lay on the ground beside him. It was a very disagreeable situation. Then suddenly he heard his name called by the captain. He got to his feet and strolled over to the group. Everybody became silent. Then Regan heard the captain say: "Take off that tape and go for your man or ..."

He knelt down and unwound the tape. There were yards of it. He could hear somebody snigger viciously on the touchline: "Oh, Lord! The baby is wearing bandages." Then the whistle blew again. A cry arose: "Come on Blackburn. Give it to them, Bill. On the toes, forwards."

The match became desperate now. Big Blackburn, the captain and the leading forward, with his skull-cap strapped around his skull and his huge arms swinging, broke away with the ball on his toes, down the centre of the field to the enemy's twenty-five. But the enemy full-back went down to the ball and then a mass of men all tumbled in a heap, struggling, until at last Blackburn's huge form arose in the centre, pushing men off him and struggling to break loose again. But they held on to his legs and back and he went down again, while the crowd cheered wildly. It was a great scene, and even Regan, shivering out on the wing, began to feel a thrill.

Away went the ball again. This time the enemy had it. They pressed up the field, passing and repassing cunningly, until they reached the home twenty-five. There was another scrum and then suddenly the ball was shot out, passed, once, twice rapidly. The right centre three-quarter got it, stood still, took deliberate aim and dropped a beautiful goal. This time the enemy team yelled and rushed around shaking one another by the hand. The home crowd on the touchlines were silent.

Again the ball was kicked off. There was only twenty minutes to go. The forwards were becoming exhausted and vicious. Several times in the next few minutes the referee had to warn

men of both sides and there were five free kicks. The struggle
became fearfully intense, and no sooner did a man get the ball
than there were two or three pouncing on him and dragging him
to the ground. The ball was kept all the time among the forwards and centres.

Then Regan got another chance to retrieve his honour. A
terrific forward rush came down the touchline towards him. He
heard the cry "Get down to it. Get down to it." He stood trembling for a moment, and then, closing his eyes, he dashed
straight forward and hurled himself on the ball, gripping it
savagely in his arms. He rolled over and over on the ground and
then a mass of men fell on him, grunting and panting, pulling
at him and pushing. He almost lost consciousness, but he lay
very still and clung to the ball. They formed over him and he was
carried along the ground almost suffocated, until at last the
refreee blew his whistle and the press broke to form a scrum.
Then he struggled to his feet. As he arose he could hear a great
cheer and a cry: "Bravo, Regan." Somebody clapped him on the
back as he sprang backwards to his position.

But he took no notice of the cheer or of the clap on the back.
He was in a fighting frenzy. This was the first time in his life he
had gone down to a forward rush. It was his first good bruising
on a hard field, and it awoke some element in him that nobody
thought he possessed, of which he himself was unaware. Standing now, leaning forward, waiting for the ball, he felt that he
wanted to fall upon the whole enemy team and lay them low.
His face was covered with earth. His right knee was skinned.
There was a big bruise on his left hip and his whole body tingled
with pain after the mauling he had received. But his heart
thumped with excitement and he felt fierce instead of feeling
afraid. Afraid! He knew he would never be afraid again.

The ball was thrown into the scrum. There was a fierce push.

The enemy got it. In a flash it was passed out to the centre, but almost before he had time to move off with it Regan had jumped clean on to his shoulders and brought him down. Another cry went up, and this time there was more wonder in the cry than joy. The ball dribbled away down the field, carried off by the home backs until play stopped again in a scrum on the home side of midfield. Ten minutes to go.

"Let it out, forwards," yelled the crowd. "Give it to Regan. Regan. Go on, Regan."

A wave of enthusiasm swept over the field and at last Regan was completely carried away by it. He felt himself a hero. And on such occasions it seems that chance also favours a man, for almost immediately Regan found himself running along, with the ball in the possession of his centre, who was running cleverly forward trying to make an opening. "Pass, pass," they cried. But he held on to it too long and he was tackled before he passed. The ball dribbled along the field and Regan had to turn back and pick it up. It seemed impossible for him to do anything with it but kick, as the whole field was now in front of him. "Find touch," somebody shouted. Regan hesitated for a moment and then decided to kick, but just as he was on the point of kicking, a forward rushed on him and again he felt a little thrill of fear at the possibility of contact with the burly figure and another fall to the ground. Suddenly, thrusting the ball under his arm, he dashed off.

The thing was so unexpected and impossible that he got ten yards ahead before there was any move made to stop him. Even his own men were amazed, because, instead of adopting his usual tactic of doubling out to the wing, he had plunged straight into the crowd, jumping like a deer and punching with his outstretched right hand. With this rush he broke through the enemy forwards and headed across the field towards the corner of the enemy goal-line. But he had still half the field to travel and the whole enemy back line doubled around to stop him. It was so unexpected that even on the touchline the fellows were silent, expecting him to be tackled every moment.

But he still went on. The scrum-half threw himself at his legs, but Regan vaulted right over the scrum-half's head and, suddenly swerving from the right centre three-quarters who were waiting for him, headed off the other way. Then the cheering began. He had still three men to pass, but he was going like a hare, swerving from right to left, jumping and punching. He reached the enemy twenty-five and then his own man came up on him from one side while the full-back approached from the other. There was a tense moment, and although the suspense lasted for only three seconds or so, it seemed a year to the fellows on the touchline who stood with their mouths open, stooping, with their caps in their hands. Then the clash came. The three men met at the same time. They all went down. But . . . Good Lord! Regan was up again and off like a shot straight for the goal-posts. He ran in at full speed, touched down without slackening speed and then raced back again, as if he had gone mad and wanted to score again at the other posts. But as soon as he reached his own men, they stopped him and slung him on to their shoulders.

But there was only a faint cheer from the touchline. Would the try be converted? The enemy was still leading. Not a sound was heard while the ball was placed. One, two, three moments. Then the ball sailed away. What? Straight through the posts. The flag went up. A wild cheer arose and then the referee blew his whistle.

Immediately the boys poured into the field over the ropes. Regan was hoisted on to Big Blackburn's shoulders and the whole school followed him to the pavilion shouting: "Re-e-e-gan! Re-e-e-gan!"

Bryan MacMahon

MY LOVE HAS A LONG TAIL

THE OLD MAN, a misty figure in a frayed overcoat, stood at a country crossroads on a morning in January. Behind him was a dripping clump of blackthorn bushes; below and around him were the rushy fields of a cutaway bog. Above his head were the underbellies of low clouds barely touched by the light of a sullen daybreak.

His cap vizor was drawn down over his small face which was dominated by askew steel-rimmed spectacles, one of the lenses of which, by the vice of being vertically cracked, made it sometimes appear that its owner had three eyes. At his knee, at the end of a loop of rusty chain, its neck encircled by a damp leather collar, its body scantily covered by a frayed dog-cover, stood a dispirited brindled and white greyhound.

From time to time the old man kept turning his face northward, to where the roadway emerged from among the grove of trees amid which the bland face of a "great house" could barely be discerned.

Time passed. The mist had changed insidiously to fine rain. As the hound began to shiver and whine the old fellow stroked

---

Bryan MacMahon was born in Listowel, Co. Kerry, where he taught for most of his working life and about which he published a best-selling autobiography in 1992. Well-known as novelist, dramatist and translator from Irish, he is also acknowledged as a master of the short story.

the animal's head, caress-covering its muzzle with a calloused
hand. He began to mumble to himself with increasing loudness
as if opposing unseen critics. He glanced back at the crouched
cabin a few hundred yards away at the end of a torn passage into
the bogland where lamplight showed wanly through a small
recessed window. "Why doesn't she go back to bed?" he said
aloud. Then still louder, "What has she to do now that I'm going
to the Sales?" In a still louder tone, as if his wife could hear at
that distance, "Why the hell, woman, don't you go back to bed?"
Then with an inconsequential snort, "Yourself and your ten
cartridges going out, to tally six birds and four cartridges comin'
back!"

A donkey and cart loomed up behind him. The ironshod
wheels of the cart had moved noiselessly on the bog-mould of the
road surface so that they were beside him almost before he
realised it. In the body of the cart stood a rusted milk-churn. A
seated figure, its legs dangling, was hunched at the intersection
of the shaft and floor of the vehicle.

"Any trace of a car to the north?" the waiting old man asked
abruptly.

The sunken figure of the man on the cart, a dirty trenchcoat
wrapped around him, slowly raised his head. "Wee!" he said
pulling on the reins. The donkey drew to a halt.

"That you, Mike?" he said in sham surprise.

"That's me, Peter! You're early for the creamery!"

"I thought I heard you . . . 'takin' stock'," the newcomer
chuckled, obviously referring to Michael's habit of speaking to
himself. He swung round as far as his cramped position would
allow. "No sign of a light to the north," he said. "If it passed Mr
Hogan's you'd have seen it," he added. Turning his head and
looking down at the hound, "You're off to the Sales?"

"I am."

"You'll be expecting a tidy penny?"

"If breedin' counts he should sell well."

"Three figures? Mebbee four?"

"If the Continentals attend, he could make any money."

There was a pause as if for savouring this piece of information.

Peering down at the hound, Peter asked, "How's he bred?"

"He's by Soirée out of Full and Plenty."

"Glover's bitch?"

"Aye."

"The dam is good."

"So is the sire."

"What's his track name?"

"Parsley Sauce."

"Damn good!" A faint teehee. After a pause, "Does he have to run some class of a trial?"

"The trial is a matter of form. Buyers can size up a good hound by looks alone."

"That's their trade! A good hound is better than a bawn of cows." Meaningfully, "But only if you're lucky." Then to the donkey, "Go on out! Tck-tck. Parsley Sauce," Peter said with a chuckle as he drove on. "Damn good."

Mike was left alone in the misty rain. Looking after the donkey cart he muttered, then spat bitterly. Light began to sieve into the morning. From the high grove around Hogan's place a cock crowed. Rooks spoke hoarsely from a few desolate trees.

Mike thrust the crosspiece of the end of the chain-lead deep into his overcoat pocket. A drop gathered at the end of his nose. He opened his mouth once to reveal toothless gums. "The bugger! With his Mr Hogan!" he said aloud. "Everyone at the creamery'll know my business now." The hound didn't look up at the sound of its owner's voice. A sidelong glance showed Mike that the lamplight no longer showed in the window of his cabin. On the ridge to the north a bright light showed in the yard of the "great house". Mike's head drooped: the hound's head dropped still lower. The chain noised so faintly that it seemed as if mist and rain had oiled it into silence. Mike could hear the rain dropping from the bushes behind him. There was the remote complaint of a morning bird.

At last the old man raised his head. He saw the reflection of headlights on the low clouds in the northern sky. Ah, here was the car topping the rise and moving through Hogan's Grove. The old man's face brightened. As he tugged on the chain the hound came dismally to life. "My love has a long tail," he said brightly as he waited for the car to draw up beside him.

The driver lowered the window and looked out. "I'm to meet a man . . ." he began, and recognizing Mike and his hound blurted, "Jesus!" Then with an explosive exclamation he made as if to drive off.

Michael clutched the edge of the car window. "It's me, Mike Lanigan!" he shouted. "'Tis me, I tell you. Me you were to meet!"

The motor-car drew to a reluctant halt. Wearily the driver said, "Too bloody well I know who it is. If I'd known it before now I'd have stayed at home in my warm bed."

"You got my message, Tom?"

"You're too feckin' fly altogether," the hackney driver said. "You got a woman to phone from the store knowin' that if you phoned yourself I'd refuse you. 'To meet a man at the Cross below Hogan's. A man who wanted to go on a drop run,'" he mimicked. "Too well I know your drop run. Where the hell is it you wanted to go anyway?"

"To the Sales in Cork."

"A three hours run! Take your hand off the car. I've had my

bellyful of you and your hounds at Trienafrinn coursing. Nearly got pneumonia loiterin' around and you blowin' your coal about all the great hounds you bred. My love has a long tail! My arse! Let go of the car, you whore's ghost, or I'll roll over you."

"Damn it, man, you can't let me down."

"I told you the last time that I was finished with you and your shaggin' hounds. It took me a solid week to wash the smell of that bloody snake out of my clean car. He all but pissed down on myself. Here, now, I warn you, take your hound out of the way or I won't be responsible for both o' you."

"Tom! Wait! Blast it for a story, it means the world and all to me. The hound is listed in the Sales. His name is in print. Don't go! I'm two years feedin' him. Just for this day. If you seen all the cows' heads I boiled for him, all the dognuts he ate, all the bread Hannie baked for him. Red meat too! We left ourselves hungry to feed him. I'm a year walkin' him in weather good and bad. I lost money to the vet to put him right. If he misses today's Sales I'll have to sell out to Hogan. Tom, myself and your father were friends. You'll only be a few hours out, I promise you that. I'll pay you well. Before God, don't let me down."

Wearily, the hackney driver slid the gear lever into neutral. In a tone of angry resignation he said, "What money is in the Bank of Ireland won't pay me for the persecution I'm goin' to get from you today. I feel it in my bones. O Holy God!" he added impiously as he looked up into the agitated face outside his window. "What time do you expect to be back?"

"We should be in Cork for ten o'clock. With a bit o' luck the dog'll be on the bench at eleven or half past. We should be back here for half past one at the very latest. The Continental buyers will be there. So I should get good money for him. Open the door in God's holy name."

Tom beat his fist on the driving wheel. "One condition!" he

shouted. "You'll sit on the back seat with your two arms around your hound. Keeping him up on your lap. He's not to touch the upholstery. I'm up to my neck in debt for the car."

"Good man, Tom!"

"I know your couple of hours."

"That I may be as dead as my father I'll make no delay."

"An' you'll lob me thirty-four pounds into my hand. An' guarantee to be back here for two o'clock at the latest."

"I'll be back. But damn it for a story, Tom – thirty-four pounds! I haven't that much money in the world."

"Watch your toes, I'm off!"

"Wait! Say thirty."

"I won't say thirty. For thirty-three, ninety-nine. Are you goin' to piss or leave the pot?"

"Right! Let me sit in and not to have us standing here perished with the cold."

"Us!" As he leaned back to open the door, the driver paused. "If he pukes in the car, out ye go."

Mike sat in the back seat, the hound cradled in his arms. His spectacles glinted in threefold light. The car door slammed shut. Glancing into the mirror the driver shouted, "Don't attempt to raise that window. I don't care if the pair of ye freeze to death. And no smokin'." He added ironically, "My love has a long tail!" The car moved off.

The hackney driver was moonfaced with full lips and protruding eyes. He obviously lacked exercise. After a time Mike and himself struck up a semi-normal relationship. They chatted on deaths and weddings, on scandals, superstitions and unsolved murders. Now and again "Don't touch that window!" the driver roared as Mike tried to take advantage of their quasi-friendship to sneak the window upwards.

Houses, villages, churches, pubs slid by in the as yet unreal light.

Now and then the greyhound whined his sense of discomfort. He even made frantic efforts to get off the knife edges of Mike's thighs; there ensued a confused flurry of arms and legs and paws in which the hound barely came off second best. Eventually the hound, resigned to his fate, sat on his perch panting and showing the purple and white insides of his mouth.

For the last twenty miles or so before entering the city the road was a series of S-hooks and horseshoe turns. The movements of the vehicle caused Mike and his hound to rock violently from side to side: there were times when the owner was sent sprawling sidelong against one or other of the doors. From time to time his lips moved either in pious prayer or picturesque obscenity.

On the outskirts of the city the emerging traffic of morning, much of it composed of heavy trucks and trailers, came thundering against them, threatening recurrently to squash the smaller vehicle as a clock-beetle is squashed under a midnight boot. The dog became agitated but Mike managed to hold on until at last before entering the city proper they saw the long palisade of corrugated iron which separated the greyhound track from the roadway. There was a great number of vehicles in the vicinity so that they were fored to park at some distance from the main gateway.

Once out of the car Mike snatched the old cover from the hound, took a folded and ironed one from the pocket of his overcoat, briskly shook it free, placed it on the back of his hound and tied its tapes around the neck and belly. From the driver's seat Tom eyed the cover with a merciless eye: it was obviously homemade, its bright yellow cloth trimmed in red with the letters ML, crudely cut from white cloth, still more crudely affixed to its right flank. The hound pricked up its ears on hearing the distant rattle whirr and whine of the electric hare, the baying of frustrated hounds, and the yells of partisans.

The enclosure was thronged with men and hounds. Huge countrymen in frieze overcoats wearing thick-soled boots clumped here and there in front of the stands, their bodies dwarfing the hounds they led. They moved towards the kennels according as their names were called to take part in the trials. When a trial was being run the waiting hounds became frenzied with excitement: once a large black hound, led by a girl of ten or so, slipped its collar, leaped the barricade and to the accompaniment of outraged shouts from the large throng of spectators took part in the race. Mike, no longer the disconsolate figure at the crossroads, suddenly became peremptory and authoritative. With a sharp word to the driver he disappeared into the crowd.

Tom sidled forward to lean against the rails bordering the track. There, he borrowed a sales list from a studious punter: he swore yet again on seeing Mike's hound was listed No. 135 – almost at the bottom of the card. He began to reckon what time it would be when he would get home. The trials already being run off in bunches of six hounds had begun at 9.30 and were due to end at 1.00 p.m. when there was a break for luncheon. That luncheon break would certainly not begin till 1.15 or 1.30; if he knew anything about the time-keeping of doggy men the sales proper wouldn't begin until a quarter to three. He now realized that Mike's hound wouldn't reach the sales table till seven or eight o'clock at night.

"The son of a bitch!" he muttered. "Himself and his drop run. I'll be lucky if I get home by midnight." He then went off to protest to his fare.

He found Mike, surrounded by his cronies, his spectacles agleam, a glass of porter in his hand, standing imperiously in the bar. Mike became supercilious when he saw the driver approaching. He was quite tolerant of Tom's attack. In his eye was the gleam of an amused gambler. He winked at his companions as if asking them to bear with him in this intrusion. But, narrowing his eyes, Tom noticed that the old fellow was in the company of town and city handlers and not among the well-dressed owners. The smallholder owner was a thing of the past, he told himself with some satisfaction.

Somewhat consoled by his conclusion, Tom returned to the enclosure where he looked around in search of the foreign buyers. He visualized them as wearing wine-coloured or beige leather jackets under camel-haired coats lined with pure wool, their splendour crowned by green velour hats with a blackcock's feather in the band. These were nowhere to be seen.

The hackney driver walked out through the main gateway and trundled to the nearest pub, which was about four or five hundred yards away. He was out of breath when he entered the empty lounge. He ordered a hot whiskey and sat back in resignation to face the wearisome day. Hannie would think he was out of his mind, he told himself, as the taste of hot whiskey, lemon and cloves pleasantly bit his tongue-tip. But where taking a phone message was concerned he had never met a woman who could take one right. He rehearsed his homecoming: "Wouldn't you have the common sense to ask who was hiring the car? Eh? Or ask where they wanted to go? Eh? Or when they expected to be back? Eh? Is it too much to ask that whenever that bloody phone rings you should ask yourself 'Who? When? Where? What? Why? and How much?' Eh?"

Much later he drained the dregs of the whiskey and returned to the track. "Second last," the punter at the rails said in answer to Tom's query as to how Parsley Sauce had fared in the trial.

* * *

At last there was movement in the enclosure. A triptych dais or desk, its front taller than its rear, had been placed in the stand nine or ten steps above the ground – this to accommodate the auctioneer, the relief auctioneer and the clerk. A low table was placed in front of this dais and three chairs set behind it – all with due solemnity. Microphone-testing over, three men advanced on the stand with the solemnity of priests entering a sanctuary. Taking his place behind the desk, the first auctioneer, his bald head glistening, his features wine-red as a consequence of a good luncheon, glared around him at the scattered crowd. He tapped his fingernails on the microphone, then as if in rage he struck the desk a resounding crack with his gavel. Instantly there was silence. All present poured out of the bar and gathered in a circle beneath the auctioneer.

Calling on the clerk to read the rules of the Sales, the auctioneer's voice roused echoes from the galvanized iron sheeting above his head. He frowned at the resonance of his own voice. The clerk began to read, quietly laying stress on the fact that as soon as he had placed his hound on the table in front of the dais each owner would whisper the reserve price to him, the clerk. This was important, he said, looking meekly down.

The assistant auctioneer retreated a step, and, with the volume adjusted, the auction proper began; the clerk's eyes as he read the bids were the darting eyes of a fox.

The Sales droned on and on. A jealous sigh went through the crowd as one hound made £2,800. About six o'clock the lights on the stand were turned on. There was now only a small knot of people left around the table. Beyond them the track seemed to extend endlessly and intimidatingly beyond the circle of wan light. Beyond the track the amber city lights glowed in aureoles of mist.

At last Tom heard Lot 135 being called. He left the rails and stood a little distance from the knot of people. He saw Mike crouching to lift the hound by its four legs and place it proudly on the table.

"Eight hundred and fifty," Mike said in a whisper to the clerk. Writing the figure the clerk rolled his eyes incredulously. The small crowd tittered. Mike's lips twitched as, proudly, he stood aside.

"What am I bid for Lot 135? Parsley Sauce! A brindled and white two-year old hound by Soirée out of Full and Plenty?"

The auctioneer went on to give the date the hound was whelped, its weight and the times of the races it had run.

Silence.

"Am I bid one hundred guineas for this son of a famous sire?"

Silence.

"Am I bid seventy-five guineas? Sixty guineas? Fifty guineas? Thirty guineas? Twenty-five, twenty-five, twenty-five – am I bid twenty-five guineas for this well-bred and well-proportioned hound?"

Silence.

"Gentlemen. Have I any bid at all? Final call, gentlemen. Any bid? No?"

Someone in the huddle sniggered. The gavel crashed down on the table. "Take him down!" the auctioneer ordered peremptorily. Then "Next lot, 136," he said with a final look of disdain.

Mike gathered the hound's legs in his arms and turned away. The lights in the stand glittered crazily on the lenses of his glasses. He staggered down the steps. He carefully set the hound on the ground and walked away. After a few paces he took the old cover from underneath his overcoat and placed it on the hound's back. The hackney driver watched him as he tied the laces on the cover. He followed Mike as he walked towards the main gate. The old fellow seemed to have aged since morning. His lips were moving. Tom braced himself against weakness.

"Hey there, Mike," he said hastening to catch up with him at the gate. "How did things go?"

Mike never slackened his stride. "You were watchin'," he said tonelessly.

The pair walked in silence towards where the car was parked. All the other cars had gone so that now it stood alone. "Did you have a bite to eat?" the driver said.

"I had a drink."

"It's a long fast," the driver said. Mike did not reply.

As he opened the door of the car, "I've a ground sheet in the boot," Tom suggested. "The hound can lie on it on the back seat. You can sit in front with myself."

"I'll go as I came!"

They drove off. Now and again where amber street lights in the villages flickered in the car Tom glanced in the mirror and saw the frozen face of the old man, sitting erect with the hound spread awkwardly across his knees. The window was closed and a strong smell of kennel pervaded the vehicle. "Smoke your pipe if you like," Tom ventured.

"I won't bother," the old man said sharply.

After travelling for some time Mike blurted, "If you seen all the meat this fellah ate!"

"That a fact?"

"If I had a gun I'd shoot him."

"That a fact?"

"We fed him like a gamecock. It cost us seven pounds a week to keep him. I went in debt for him."

After a pause the old man's voice tailed off into inaudibility.

The driver sniffed. The smell of the car-heater, the smell of liniment, the smell of hot hound.

"Still an' all . . . " Mike began afresh.

"Eh?"

"If he got a fair crack o' the whip he'd have hammered the field. I know that in my heart. The favourite tried to savage him goin' in the wicket. I breed racers, not fighters. The man on the traps − he gave 'em a long slip − my fellah hates that. To cap everything he got a bump at the first bend and was crowded out at the last. Easy for the favourite to win when he had every dog cowarded before the race began."

"That a fact?"

"If they ran them trials fair, there'd be five lengths of light between this lad and the rest of the field."

"What about the Continentals?"

"The airport in Holland was closed with fog. The home crowd had the buyin' all to themselves. They had puffers drivin' up the prices for their chums. I wasn't the only one that was grumblin'." A long pause.

They were passing through a village.

"Will you take a word of advice?" the driver asked.

"What is it?"

"Get out of hounds altogether!"

"You must be mad! How would you like it if I told you to get out of cars?"

"If you're rich an' you want to be poor, keep a horse, a hound and a whore."

"Nonsense, man! Did you hear about O'Dea the ex-schoolmaster? Made six and a half thousand on his first hound. And what about the Mangan boy at the Lots whose dog sired the winner of the Irish Purse? Isn't he minting money out of the service. An' the woman in Oohashla who made a fortune out of one belly o' pups?"

"A middlin' hound is a curse from God."

"A good hound is a gift of the Almighty."

"A middlin' hound'd break Rockefeller."

"A good hound is like winnin' the Sweepstake."

"Take my advice! Forget your hounds!"

"I will not forget my hounds! You're a townie, so what do you know about the countryside at break o' day? The line of light in the east. The first stirring of the birds. We steppin' together, him and me. Muscle forming on his hindquarters as his body sheds fat. His motions those of a healthy hound. Then, when the time comes, there's the brace of hounds in slips. The hare goin' up the field. The hounds pullin' the slipper after them. Yeh, yeh, yeh! Who can whack that? Eh? Before I die I hope to own a hound that'll make the whole of Ireland ring with my name."

"There's no affection to a hound."

"The way his legs move are affection enough for me. My love has a long tail."

They came to the crossroads where they had first met. Beyond the bogland was the small square of light in the window of the crouched cottage. Through the rookery trees, far above from Hogan's place, the yard light shone.

"What'll I be givin' you?" Mike asked.

"What we bargained for – thirty-four pounds."

"You'll leave me without my supper."

"Better you than me. You have your dream of Clounanna Altcar or Biscayne: I have my dream too – to educate six children."

"What you're asking is out of all reason."

"It's now ten o'clock at night. I'm with you since seven this morning. If I was paid by time 'twould cost you the most of a hundred quid. Wait'll I put on the roof light. Finger your fob like a good man. An' don't ask me for a luckpenny – that day is gone. That's it, thirty-three, thirty-four." With a laugh, "By right it should be guineas! Don't fall into the dyke. Slam the door easy."

"Good luck whatever. Wait – if you're asked, say I refused good money."

"I'll do that! Good luck, now. Don't forget – give up the shaggin' hounds."

The car moved off leaving Mike alone in the drizzle and the dark. He stood irresolute for a moment or two. The bogland stretched for miles around him. As he began to rehearse aloud what he would say to his wife a figure materialized from behind a clump of furze on the roadside.

"Oaah, Mike!" – as if he had been waiting for a long time.

Grumpily, "That you, Peter?"

Craftily, "Aye." A pause. "Did you sell?"

"I could have sold, an' sold well. But I wasn't going' to let him go at what was offered."

"That was a tidy figure, I'd say?"

"Close to what I expected. But not the whole way."

"You'll stick it out for the . . . " Peter put up four fingers.

"These buckoes took my name an' address. They have big cars. They'll likely be nosin' around here one of these days."

"How did the trial go?"

"Trials are a matter of form. It's breedin' they judge by."

"The Continentals?"

'Every class, creed an' denomination was there!"

"They'll give down the prices in the paper on Thursday. And the buyers too. Was that Tommy Dufficy was drivin' you?"

"It could have been one of the Dufficys, all right."

"You're tired now. And hungry no doubt."

"Tired? An' a new car under me? Hungry? An' lashin's of meat pies on the track?"

"What did he charge you for the car?"

"He'll make out the mileage, an' let me know when I'm in town."

"My sister'll be wantin' him the day after tomorrow. A funeral in Tullabeg. I might travel myself. Parsley Sauce," he muttered with a chuckle as he drifted away.

"The bastard!" Mike swore, having ensured that Peter was out of earshot. "And a spy for Hogan! He's after sellin' his own holding, keepin' only a life interest. Now he wants every fox to have a burned tail like himself."

The hound beside him, Mike squelched along the road towards the opening to the boggy passage that led to his cottage. "Give up hounds!" he muttered, then raising his voice, "My love has a long tail." He stopped and fumbled in his pocket. "One pound between me and pension day. I was to bring back tea, sugar and bread. Hannie'll have to do without. I'll have cold tongue for supper." He laughed bitterly.

He walked a few steps, then came to a stop. Looking up in the direction of Hogan's he said, "Big farmers gettin' bigger by the minute. I'd make money if I let my turf banks. But once in you couldn't get them out. I'll hold out as long as I can. I was sure the sale of the hound would tide me over till herself was of pension age. Then we'd be secure. My father lived through hard times. My grandfather was an evicted tenant. My great-grandfather weathered the Famine. We always lived close to the ground."

He stood and looked around to ensure there was no one to hear. He raised his voice a little.

"Peasants they called us – the big bugs. But wars went over our heads. We lived where they died. We lived because we had the firin', the home bacon, the spuds, the fowl and the eggs. The milk too – even if it was goat's milk itself. Spring water, the rabbit, the hare, the salmon, the white trout, a handful of vegetables – maybe a few stools of rhubarb. I never attended a doctor in my life: we always had our own cures. Mebbe I should have gone to Birmingham like the rest. But I was sticky. I tried to escape by the short cut of the hound. Are there fellahs like me in other lands? In lands where the rain and puddle doesn't make them crazy like they make us here? Big bugs like Hogan waitin' to gobble up small lads like me. Castles fallin' and dung-hills risin'. The Troubles! All they signified was swappin' masters. Martin's store at the crossroads − I don't blame him for pressin' me for what I owe. He's on the way out too − the supermarkets in the towns are sucking him dry. Up to this I paid as I went. Now I'm in a hobble."

He stood on the high road-edge. The wind whined. The dog whined. The bushes dripped.

"I'm not the only one is mad. All Europe is mad. The town market is gone. The fair is no more. The creamery is a thing of the past. A factory takes their place. All their eggs in one basket, an' if that basket falls what then − eh? Stone mad! If my Hannie sells six eggs to a house in town she's likely to get a process. If she dares sell a pound of home butter she's liable to end up in court. If she kills and draws a pullet and offers it to a customer she'll get a food prosecution. Is that madness? Yes or no? Answer me!" His voice was loud now.

The wind. The whining of the hound. The drip of rain.

"If all goes to all the Council'll bury me." After a pause his voice altered to self-pity. "What am I now but a queer old fellah in the back seat of a car with a hound across my knees and lights flashin' on my face? I'm a class of a clown in a circus. An' yet, in spite of all, I'll hold to one creed till I go into the box. My love has a long tail! Take that from me and I'm no man. Let them jeer when they hear me sayin' it. My love has a long tail!" he shouted.

Craftily his voice lowered as again he began to mutter: "Then again if I sold the hound well the pension officer might come down on Hannie when she applies. A peasant! What was Pope John but a peasant? Straight up out of the cowdung like myself. He had big ears like the old people I knew around here when I was young."

Mike stood in reverie at the mouth of the tattered passage that led down to his cabin. He heard the mighty night with its fugitive stars assert itself around him. His senses probed it in a great ring, deciphering its minuscule noises, the antennae of his perceptions moving outwards, then swinging round the landscape almost in a complete circle. His nostrils flared as he inhaled the sulphurous odour of the black turf banks and the winter heather. There was a cry of a night-bird and the yelp of an animal in the dark; then from far down to the right came a mocking call of "Cuckoo!" and again "Cuckoo!"

That would be Peter, taunting him, Mike told himself quietly. Though his tormentor was surely half a mile away, he fancied he could see his leering face and his hand cupped about his mouth. The peasant was treacherous even where his fellow peasant was concerned. Mike could interpret the call. "You're takin' stock," it jeered, "and now you have damn all to take stock of!" The call roused him to a slow anger. His mouth worked. His nostrils opened and closed.

"Peter, you bastard of a spy," he jerked aloud as if the other could hear him, "I'll best you yet." Then turning to address others in an imaged audience, "You too, Hogan, bastard of a big farmer up there on the hill ready to gobble up my few acres. And you bastard of a driver, Tom, that bled me white. Ye bastards at the track who put me last on the list. You bastard of an auctioneer and your penciller with the eyes of a fox. Ye bastards standin' around that gave no bid or that puffed when it suited. Ye bastards from Amsterdam that never turned up. You bastard at the traps with your long slip. You bastard at the store pressing me to pay. Ye bastards in Brussels who won't let us live! Ye're nothing but a pack of bastards, the lot of ye. But before the face o' Christ I'll beat ye all yet!"

The cottage door dragged along the floor as it was being

opened from the inside. The dim square of light above the out-side half-door was flawed by the upper part of the body of a smallish woman. Her head seemed permanently twisted to one side so that the grey bun of hair on her poll could barely be discerned. Leaning her forearms on the ledge of the half-door, she waited.

Mike braced himself. He lifted his small crowded face with its glinting glasses. He wiped the froth from his mouth corners with the back of his hand. Then, leading his hound, he squelched across the quaking bridge of sods and bogdeal as he moved down towards the crouched form of his waiting wife.

Mary Morrissy

THE BUTTERFLY

SWIMMING, LAWLOR the coach said, is about honour not skill. His philosophy of swimming was meant to comfort boys like me in the club who would never be champions, although I suspected, even then, that he secretly despised our kind. I had been sent to swimming classes on the advice of our family doctor after several bouts of pneumonia. I had what was known in the trade as a "shoemaker's chest" so that from breast bone to belly button, where others were firm and hard, I had a disconcerting hollow. I was also fat, with white whale-like thighs that rubbed together giving rise to ire.

"The swimming will expand his lungs and will get rid of some of that flab," the doctor said, winking at my mother and poking me in the ribs where he met only flaccid pouches of skin. Fat children, regardless of their ailments, rarely excite sympathy.

At eleven, I was the oldest in the beginners' class.

My father, who could not swim himself, sat in the smelly public gallery looking down at me, with nothing more than duty written on his face. He remained non-committal throughout

---

Mary Morrissy was born in Dublin. She is on the staff of the Irish Times, *and won a Hennessy Literary Award in 1984. She has published a collection of short stories,* A Lazy Eye.

those tortured Sunday afternoons while I thrashed around in the shallow end of the municipal baths.

I remmber to this day their smell of dampness, and of dirt thinly disguised with chlorine – that same mix of brutalised cleanliness that piss and disinfectant make in public lavatories. For me it is the smell of terror, the clutch of fear at the base of a child's stomach. Butterflies, they call it. But they were no mere butterflies for me; they were dangerous lumbering animals gnawing away at my innards. I always seemed to be shivering, before, during and after the swimming class. And despite having swallowed a gallon of the eerie-green water, my mouth was always dry. The shrieks of terror – or is it delight? – of children at the seaside, rising and falling with the waves, always bring that time back to me. There is a blood-curdling sanctity in those cries, as if it were their very souls calling out.

There were pleasant sensations too, of course. Sloshing through the foot bath, our only protection against verrucas. The great shards of relief stepping into the shower afterwards against a backdrop of teeming voices. Standing there with toes and fingers shrivelled white from the cold knowing the ordeal was over for another week. The feeling of damp limbs in warm, dry clothes. And how good everything tasted after a swim! And there was Kay. Kay made the lessons almost bearable. She was Lawlor's daughter, and one of the brightest stars of the Chrysalis Club. She trained with the under sixteen boys relay team. Roped off from us, these boys flexed themselves at the pool's edge, their chests broad and firm, shapely muscles in their forearms, their crotches bulging and forests of hair on their shins. Under Lawlor's eye, they ploughed through the water, their backs gleaming like the rumps of porpoises. He stood at the far end of the pool, bellowing at them while smoothing drops away from his twill trousers and balding pate.

Kay was thirteen when I started swimming first. After finishing her training in the deep end she would help Miss Dignam out with the beginners. She would hold me, the light touch of her palm in the small of my back, the damp tendrils of her hair escaping from her tight cap and touching my cheek and brow. I had never been so close to a girl before. The sleek feel of her blue swimsuit, with flecks of what seemed like silver in it – but was, of course, lycra – began to send a different kind of shiver through me. I would clutch onto her firm, thin arms, looking up trustingly into her hazel eyes as she pulled me gently across the pool. Shoals of beginners came and went while I stayed, blissful, in the shallows with Kay – dark, quivering Kay – her tender urgings of "kick, kick," in my ear as we swayed in the afterswell of the boys relay team. As my infatuation grew, I realised that if I lifted my reluctant feet from the floor of the pool and floated free, I would have to sacrifice her whisperings for her father's hoarse commands.

It is easy now to look back and scoff affectionately at such infatuation, which is both more and less than love. More, because it demands nothing, expects nothing but the mere crumbs thrown unknowing from the beloved's table, and less, because it is rarely tested; it thrives in its own vacuum. But it also gives us a chance for nobility which "real" love rarely does, a chance for the fine, private gesture which our grubby everyday lives don't allow. The dilemma with Kay was that although I wished to please her by making progress, I knew that when I did I would be banished forever to the deep end. For once, my congested chest worked to my advantage, and granted me a stay of execution. An infection laid me low in the early summer and then developed into pneumonia which landed me once again in hospital. My mother, usually the delivering angel, sat at my bedside brushing my hair back from my damp forehead. For her visits she wore an expression of pitying appeal, knowing all the time that I would never yield up a corresponding measure of her generous sentiment.

"I don't know about all the swimming," she said to me. "I wonder if it's really good for you." I felt a sharp pang of alarm.

"Please, Mother, let me go back, I've nearly learned, I'm nearly there," I protested.

She smiled at me wanly.

I associate that hospital ward with the most delectable of fantasies. The speckled, tiled floor, the silver paint flaking off the iron bedstead, the bowl of bruised apples on the locker became touchstones for all sorts of flights of fancy. A shipwreck. Kay on the prow, I in the water tossing about in huge, angry waves, going down for the third time . . . Kay, fully-clothed, leaping in to save me. Safely dry-docked in bed I dreamed of returning to the squalid pool, having forgotten even the basics of swimming, to be coaxed back into life by Kay, to be held in those downy arms again.

It was a good six months before I made it back. I undressed, nervous as a bridegroom, inhaling greedily the familiar rotting smell of the cubicle. I was humming with anticipation. But when I stepped out, resplendent in a new pair of togs, I discovered that Kay had deserted the shallows. When I asked where she was I was told she didn't have time for beginners anymore, that she was training seriously for the annual gala, the glamour event between our club and The Grey Seals. Sometimes I would catch a glimpse of her finely arched arm in the water as she turned at the rope, but that was all. I plunged into the water with a vengeance. My father shot to his feet in the gallery, open-mouthed. Within a month I was making quick jerky spurts across the shallow end, breaking the waters in an impressive show of spray, if not style. I had been such a slow learner that when I staggered uncertainly down to the deep end that Sunday in October, the *real* swimmers welcomed me with a round of applause. I was scanning their faces in search of Kay when a large body detached itself from the crowd and rushed forward, crushing me in a nest of warm red flesh. I looked up and there were those same pale eyes, the springing damp curls. But something had changed, something had happened to her. She was bigger for a start, taller, fatter even. But it was more than that. She had developed breasts. Huge breasts. I knew, of course, that women – women like my mother – had breasts, or at least protrusions up there. But I had always thought they had something to do with having babies, or with being a "woman". But Kay was not a woman, was she? I watched, horrified, as she jumped into the pool, treading water below me and beckoning to me to dive in and join her. I stood looking down at what I remember as a vertiginous chasm between her breasts, the slight displacement of the cups of her new swimsuit revealing the tender white parts which had not been touched by the sun. I could not bear to look any longer. I was afraid I might fall in . . .

Kay still fussed over me but it was never quite the same. I was still in love with her, but pity had crept in somewhere, pity for those great breasts she had been lumbered with. And I realised that while I was daydreaming in hospital, some vital clue which would have made this change more understandable had been handed out, and I had missed it.

The day of the big gala came. I was not competing so I sat with my father in the gallery. Watching from that height I could enjoy Kay's smooth strokes – her forté was the front crawl and her great shelf was submerged in the writhing foam. For a moment, as her slender hand made the winning touch on the bar, I loved her again as before. But it was only momentary. The minute she hauled herself out of the pool, tiny rivulets rolling down her cleavage, the feeling evaporated. But my moment of glory – or was it honour? – was yet to come. Towards the end of the gala, the under twelve butterfly final was announced. The Grey Seals had two competitors but our club's swimmer, a tall, thin freckled boy, had come down with the measles. Mr. Lawlor called out on the microphone for a volunteer. Kay was up by my side, still wet from her race and heaving from the exertion.

"You'll do it, won't you, Canice?" she pleaded. "We must have someone or else we'll lose on points. You're the only one . . ."

"But I can't do the butterfly," I wailed, the old terror re-emerging.

"There's nothing to it," she said. "Just legs and arms together, like this." She gestured, her arms spread in a wide arc, her breasts slapping noisily together.

"*Please*, Canice, for me."

I was shunted into a pair of trunks, too big for me on top so that they had to be tied up with a safety pin. The race is a blur to me now, but the butterfly suited me. I kicked and thrashed around and found myself moving. As I lifted my head out of the water for air, I heard the frenzied roar of the crowd which seemed to blossom into one great damp undulation of fogged sound. Through a cloud of water I saw their waving arms and swift streaks of colour, before being submerged again. I came last, but since there were only three competing I won the bronze medal, limping home, exhausted, after three lengths. Kay was there at the finish, leaning eagerly over the edge, extending a hand to haul me out, her face moist and smiling.

She is frozen there at that moment as if the shutter of my memory had suddenly whined into action. There must have been other days, other moments of nectar with Kay at their centre, but if there were, they have faded completely away, as if she was a character killed off early in a play. Now, only the distortions remain. I was a small boy then and things seemed bigger than they actually were. Poor Kay has become, in retrospect, something of a side-show freak in my memory — The Fat Lady, small hands clasped on her hips, preening at her own enormous, placid girth. But residues of the feeling still linger. I avoid watching gymnastics on television, for example. The sight of those rubbery pubescent girls, their bodies spare and certain yet with a promise of softness to come, can bring on a strange rush of emotion, and the sad, bewildering flavour of loss.

Donn Byrne

"IRISH"

EASTWARD THE LINE of Twenty-fourth Street flowed
evenly like a sluggish river, hazy, dim, antique, mottled
by the lights of the little shops, of blotches and shafts of yellow
illumination from the glass panels of the old houses, iron railings, and small scrofulous gardens. Past the old houses,
at the juncture of Seventh Avenue and the street, came an
irregular blaze, a sort of ochre ray from a cellar where an Italian
had a coal, ice, and wood business; the glare of the cigar-
store; the thin ray of the news-stand kept by the fat, rather
dirty, old German woman; the pale, sinister windows of the
Chinese restaurant, and the arrogant blaze from Slavin's
saloon.

At no time did the street appear so well as it did now, in the
dusk of the early New York spring. The darkness, which was
not full darkness but a sort of blue mantle, threw a veil of
illusion over it, and through the veil the lights came softly.
Before the dusk it was crude realism, and when night fell there
would be sinister shadows. But now it had a little beauty. It was

*Donn Byrne was born in New York in 1889. He was brought back by
his parents to their South Armagh home when he was a baby. He
started to write after his return to New York in 1911 and his stories
were published in leading U.S. magazines. He was killed in a car crash
in West Cork in 1928.*

like a picture a painter might have done some centuries ago, an unimportant and rather brutal picture, and time and grime and proper lighting had given it such value that one would pause before it for an instant, not knowing why the charm.

The old man sitting in the doorway of one of the little houses with the yellowish patch of grass surrounded by a warped iron railing hated the street, with the dull, cold hatred of old men. Yet he couldn't get away from it. Often his son had suggested, and his wife when she was alive had suggested, that they move to the country. "Yerra, do ye call that country?" he had snarled at the mention of Westchester, and Long and Staten Islands; and that had killed the suggestion, and they had tried to have him move up-town, to Harlem, but, "Yerra, what would I be doing up there?" he had rasped. The son had spoken of the pleasant places in Brooklyn, out Flatbush way. "Yerra, is it Brooklyn?" What impression he had of that worthy borough is hard to imagine, but he spoke with devastating contempt.

The truth was, the old man was wedded to Twenty-fourth Street. He was like some of his race who have ancient, uncomely wives whom they despise and hate but without whom they cannot live. There was the place it was fated for him to be. There was the shop where he got shaved every morning. There was the saloon where he had his three drinks a day, regular as the clock – one before lunch, one before dinner, and one before he went to bed. There was the news-stand where he snapped the daily paper from the hands of the old German woman. If an elevated train on Seventh Avenue were late, he would notice it. He had decided to be there, and there he remained.

To the eye the old man was a forbidding, a cold figure. It was more this forbidding and cold quality that made him old, rather than years. He could not have been much over fifty. But this fixity of habit, this impression of being a monument, had endowed him with antiquity. He was not a big man, but he gave the impression of size, of importance. His hair was grey, and that gave him dignity. His eye was of a colourless, aloof blue, the blue of ice. His gaunt, clean-shaven face had something ecclesiastical about it. His clothes were always a decent and expensive black, and a heavy gold watch-chain spanned his vest. He had always a stick by his side. His shoes were good and roomy, and somewhat old-fashioned. His hat was of black, hard felt, not a Derby, nor yet a high hat, but one of those things that suggest property and respectability, and somehow land. His name was Mr. McCann.

The social standing of Mr. McCann on Twenty-fourth Street was something of a phenomenon. Everyone accorded him a sort of a terrified respect. The Italian coal-and-wood man; the German news-dealer; the man in the cigar-store where he indulged in his only vulgarity, plug tobacco, which he cut with a penknife and crumbled in the palm of his hand; the bartender in Slavin's who fixed his drinks to a nicety and had a cheery and respectful "Well, Mr. McCann?" for his each entry. The street recognised he was of them, but immensely superior. He was not a gentleman, so the respect was not from caste to caste but something much more real. None ever became familiar with him, nor would any sane man think of insulting him. Aloof and stern, with terrible dignity, he moved through the street. Even the children hushed as he drew near.

None in the street ever examined their hearts or minds as to why he was paid their tribute of respect. If they had they would have found no reason for it, but they would have paid it to him all the same. He was Mr. McCann.

And this was all the more strange because he was father of Irish Mike McCann, between whom and the middle-weight boxing championship of the world there stood only two men. Irish they loved; were proud of. But it wasn't to the father of Irish that the respect was paid. It was to Mr. McCann.

A very strange thing about Mr. McCann was this: that he could only know time and space and circumstances in relation to himself. As thus: Seventh Avenue was not Seventh Avenue to him, a muscular, grimy street that plodded for a space on the west side of Manhattan, crashed northward through the Twenties, galloped toward Forty-second, crossed Broadway recklessly, and at Fifty-ninth meeting the armed front of the park, died. To Mr. McCann it was only an artery that crossed his street. Also, winter was not winter, not the keenness of frost, the tumbling, swirling miracle of the snow, but just the time when he put on his overcoat. Not did summer mean the blossoming of the boughs to him nor the happy population on the river and the beach, and the little Italians with their ice-cream carts, nor children crooning over great segments of watermelon, but just a time when it was oppressively hot. And great national events only marked points in his life. He would not say, for instance, that he was married about the time of the war with Spain, but that the Maine was sunk about the time he was married.

All his life was under his eyes, like a map one knows perfectly – a rectangular pattern. There were no whorls, no arabesques. There were no delicate shadings, no great purple splash, but precise black and white. There were no gaps he had jumped to be a mystery in his latter years. All was evident.

He could see himself in his boyhood on the Irish hills, among the plain farmer family he was born of. He could place his father, plain old tiller of the soil, always smoking a clay pipe; his mother, warm-hearted, bustling, a great one for baking bread; his brothers and sisters, honest clods. But he himself seemed to have been born superior, was superior. There was no mystery. It was a fact. He accepted it. And from him his mother accepted it.

And by his mother it was impressed on the whole family that their son and brother Dennis was superior. For him better clothes, easier work, and when he decided that farm life was not for him, no objection was made to the sending of him to college in Cork. But after a couple of years there he had made no progress with studies, and it seemed to him that the studies were not worth while. And he returned home.

They had tried to get a Government office for him then, a very small one. But that also required examinations, which he did not seem able to pass. So that a great contempt for books grew up within him. And then he grew convinced that Ireland had not enough opportunity for him. And the family got the money to send him to America.

The years at the college in Cork had intensified his sense of superiority, so that when he came to America he felt that the Irish he met there were a very inferior people. And nothing about the city pleased him; everything was much better in Ireland, he decided, and he said Ireland was a wonderful country – the only thing wrong with it was the people. And the queer thing about it was that the Irish in New York agreed with him. His few years at Cork gave them the impression he had accumulated learning, and the race has a medieval respect for books and writing.

"True for you, Mr. McCann, true for you," they would answer his remarks on the inferiority of the Irish Irish. "But what can you expect, and the centuries of oppression they have been under?"

"If they had independence enough, there would have been no oppression." "Ay, there's a lot in what you say, Mr. McCann."

His superiority disarmed them, cowed them. If one of

themselves, or a foreigner, had uttered the words, I can imagine the rush, the dull thud, the door being taken from its hinges, the mournful procession to the widow's house.

This aloofness, this superiority helped him, or, rather, made him, in the business he had chosen – life-insurance. The wisdom he uttered about life and death to a race who considers life only as the antechamber of eternity impressed his hearers, and they were afraid, too, not to take out policies from this superior, frigid, and evidently authoritative young man.

His superiority also brought him a wife, a timid, warm-hearted girl who brought a tidy sum of money as a fortune, which he spent upon himself.

She was terrified of him and very much in love with him for years. And then the love went and the terror remained. She bore him three children, two sons and a daughter. And in due time she died. But not until life had run pleasantly and respectfully for her husband, for all that he despised it, not as vanity and affliction of spirit but as inferiority and irritation.

And one son died, and a while after her mother's death Moyra, the daughter ran away, contracting a very inferior marriage with a brakeman on the Pennsylvania Railroad. And the time came when the old man had to retire from the field of insurance, new methods, new companies coming in. The native Irish died of consumption and pneumonia, and the Irish-Americans cared not a tinker's curse for superiority. So his kingdom vanished. And Poles, and French, and Italians, and the folk who came from Palestine by way of Russia, and even Chinese, jostled him. And he was left with a great sense of superiority and a growing sense of futility and one son, "the brilliant Irish-American middle-weight contender for the world's championship, 'Irish' Mike McCann!"

All that was needed now, the old man felt, to crown a useful

and superior life was a material reward. Money he didn't care
for — he had all he wanted, decent clothes, a house, tobacco,
his three drinks a day; and *The Advocate*, an Irish weekly he
read for news of people in Cork, puzzling out this genealogy and
that. As, for instance, he would read of a Patrick Murphy fined
for drunkenness at Youghal, and he would say: 'I wonder, now,
would that be a son of ould James Murphy of Ballinure. Sure,
I wouldn't put it past him. A damned drunken family they
always were." Or a name in litigation would strike him. "Them
Hamiltons were always the ones for going to law. A dirty connection!" If a pier or a piece of public property was being built,
his comment was: "I wonder who's getting the money out of
that." If a political speech were reported, he would sneer:
"Yerra, John Redmond and them fellows ought to be ashamed
of themselves, and them plundering the people, with their
tongue in their cheek." *The Advocate* was a great comfort to
him.

He often thought, as he was reading it, of how much he would
like to return to Ireland and show the ignorant the fruits of a
superior life led in hard work and wisdom. But for that he would
have to show something tangible — even money would not be
enough, so queer those people were. To impress them at all he
would have to have a title of some kind: Alderman, or Judge, or
Sheriff, "the Honourable Dennis McCann," and to have that he
would need to have gone into politics, and that was not a career
for him. To succeed there he would have to be able to mix with
the common people, drink with them, be hail-fellow-well-met
with a crowd of the dirtiest kind of Irish. No, he could never
have done that.

No, but his son might have. Sure, why couldn't he? Wasn't he
reared right among them? And though he came from a superior
house, sure, that would only be an advantage. They would look

up to him as well as be friends with him. And with the brains
he ought to have, considering his father, there was no office in
the land for which he couldn't be fitted. Surrogate, or mayor, or
governor, even! What was to prevent him if he'd been the sort
of child he ought to have been?

And if he had been that, there would have been a monument
for the old man. There would have been a justification for his
life – not that he felt he needed any, but just to show. And
people would have recognised how much the young one owed
to the old one. Then he could have gone back to Ireland for a
visit; he wouldn't have stayed there; it was a good country to
come from, as he always said. But even the ignorant common
people would have given him credit. He could hear them now
talking to his son: "Ah, sure, if your Honour's father had had
the chances you had, sure it isn't Mayor of New York he'd be,
but President of America." "Yerra, 'tis easy to see where you got
the brains, my lad. A chip of the ould block." "Dennis McCann's
son and him Governor of the Empire State. Well, you can thank
God for your father, my ould boyo."

There would have been an evidence for him, an evidence he
was entitled to.

And look you the dirty trick had been played on him. Instead
of the son who would crown his grey hairs with honour, who
would justify him, he was father to a common prize-fighter, a
man who was not looked on with respect by any. The idol,
perhaps, of the New York Irish, but of the ignorant Irish. True
he was a good boy; he didn't drink. But neither did his father
except in reason. He was generous with his money, but, after all,
what was money? Always smiling, always laughing. "Sonny"
they called him and "Irish"; that was no way to attain dignity.
Even the Italian coal-ice-and-wood man called him "Irish." The
old man would like to see anyone call himself "Irish."

And he couldn't listen to any reason. The old man had an opening for him in business up-town. A friend of his, an undertaker,
a very superior man who only did the best kind of trade, had
offered young Michael a chance. But the prize-fighter had laughed.
"In a way I'm in that line of business myself. Why change?"
The old man had shaken with rage.

"Get out of my sight, you impertinent pup!"

What were they thinking of him in Ireland at all, at all? Someone, of course, would write home and tell all about it. And if his
name, that should be treated with respect, came up, someone
would laugh: "Ould Dennis McCann! Ah, sure, what's he
anyway? Sure, his son's only a common fighter."

He could never get away from it; was never let get away from
it. Why, even tonight now, not a half-mile away, at Madison
Square Garden, Michael was fighting. And a great fuss they were
making about it, too. Some Italian he was fighting, and if he
won he was to get a fight with the champion. He'd probably win
– he always did – and beat the champion too. And the end of
it would be the honourable name would be dragged more
through the dirt of the newspapers.

"I wonder will he forget to bring home *The Advocate*," the old
man thought. "He'd better not."

Before the bell had gone for the first round, before the referee
had called them together for instructions, before even the gloves
were laced on him, Irish knew he was a beaten man.

Below him – he could see from his corner of the ring – the
great Garden was packed, a yellowish-grey foam of faces above
the dark liquid of bodies. Above those the galleries were great
ovals lined with faces. And here and there were little tendrils of
smoke. And the red caps of attendants. And occasionally the
flash of metal buttons as police and firemen hovered in the aisles.

And at the shelf round the ringside reporters with their pencils and paper, and telegraphers with their clicking instruments. The timekeeper, fingering watch and gong. In another corner of the ring the thin, lugubrious referee – himself once a famous lightweight. And everywhere lights, that in a minute or so would go out, and there would be only a great blue one over the ring. And over the house was the rippling hush that at any instant would burst into a great volume of cheers; a deep roar as of gunnery.

Across the ring, in his corner, the Italian middle-weight lolled, chattering with his seconds. Irish could occasionally glimpse the olive body; the dark hair and eyes; the even, grim face, unmarked save for the marred left ear and the minute flattening of the nose.

". . . between the leading contenders of the world's middle-weight championship, Nick Chip" [so they had Americanised Niccolo Chiapetta] "of Buffalo, and Irish Mike McCann . . ." and the rest of the sentence was lost in the roar of the Garden.

As he came to the centre of the ring for the referee's instructions, to hear interpreted the rules aginst hitting while holding, and about what was and what was not a clinch, he studied the alert, smiling Italian. Yes, Chip was far and away the best man he had ever met; too good for him, much too good. If he had only waited a year, waited six months, even; five or six months more of stiff, good fighting and he could have taken the Italian easily. A little more experience and a little more confidence if he could only have waited.

But he couldn't wait; he couldn't afford to. Neither he nor the old man could afford to.

They shook hands and returned to their corners. The whistle blew, ordering the seconds out.

"Don't box him, Irish. Stay with him. Get in close and when

you get him open, bam! See, just bam!" Old Maher, his trainer, whispered as he ducked out. "See, no fancy stuff. Just sock him. How are you feeling, Irish?"

"Fine."

"Good lad!"

Bong-g-h! He turned and walked to the centre of the ring.

The Italian had dropped into his usual unorthodox pose. His open right glove fiddling gently at the air, his left arm crooked, the glove resting against his left thigh. He moved around the ring gently, like a good woman dancer. About him was an immense economy of movement. He seemed wide open – a mark for any boxer's left hand. But Irish knew better. The Latin would sway back from the punch and counter like lightning. The old champion was wise to lie low and not to fight this man until he was compelled to.

If he could only spar him into a corner and rush him there, taking the punches on the chance of smashing him on the ropes . . . But the Italian glided around like a ghost. He might have been some sort of a wraith for shadow-boxing, except for the confident, concentrated eyes.

A minute's fiddling, shifting of position, light sparring. The creaking of the boards, the *shuff-shuff-shuff* of feet.

"Ah, why don't you walk in and kill him, Irish? He's only a Guinea!" came a voice from the gallery.

"He's a yellow. He's a yellow, da Irish," an Italian supporter jeered.

"Irish" could wait no longer. He feinted with his left, feinted again. The left shot out, missed the jaw, came home high on the head. The right missed the ribs and crashed on the Latin's back. A punch jarred Irish on the jaw. An uppercut ripped home under his heart. At close quarters the Italian was slippery as an eel. The Garden roared delight at the Irish lad's punches, but Irish knew they were not effective. And the Italian had hurt him; slightly, but hurt him.

A spar, another pawing rush; light, smart blows on the ropes. "Break! break!" the cry of the referee. Creaking of ropes and whining of boards. A patter of applause as the round came to an end. A chatter of voices as the light went up. The clicking of telegraph instruments.

"That's it! Keep after him," Maher greeted. As he sat down in his corner Irish was grim. Yes, the Italian was too good for him; he had been afraid of this: that the Italian would outgeneral him into attacking all the time. A little more experience, the fights that mean a hundred times the theory, and he would have lain back and forced Chip to stand up and face him instead of sniping him on the run. The confidence of six or seven more fights and it wouldn't have mattered to him what the gallery was shouting, what the ringside thought. He could have made Chip stand up and fight, and in a round or so the Garden would have been with him.

If only he had had a little more experience – if only he had been able to wait!

Ah, well, what was the use of grousing! He was here to fight.

"Can't you rough him up a little in the clinch, Irish?" Maher whispered.

"No, I'll fight him fair."

"Just a little to get his goat."

"No."

The lights went out, leaving only the great glare of the ring. The whistle blew; clatter of buckets and bottles. The seconds clambered down. The gong clashed shudderingly. The second round.

He walked slowly forward over the white canvas under the bluish-white arc-light, to meet his man, and then suddenly from his walk he jumped, as some jungle thing might jump. He jumped without setting, without any boxer's pose. Right for the poised, alive body he jumped. And his hands hooked for drive and uppercut. He could feel the sense of shock as they both went home, but to unvital points. The left hand thudded on the neck. The right crashed on the Italian's left arm. He was in close now, driving short lefts and rights to the body, but he was handling something that bent and sprang back like a whalebone, that moved, swayed with suppleness like some Spanish or Argentine dancer, and soon elbows locked his arms subtly, and he could do nothing.

"Come on, break!" The referee was trotting about the ring like a working terrier. Peering, moving from right to left. "Break! Break!" His voice had the peculiar whine of a dog on a scent.

He stood back, sparred a moment. Again Irish rushed. He felt on either side of his face sharp pains as of slaps with the open hand on the cheeks. Irritating things. He could feel the Latin shake as the left hand caught him flush on the ear. A tattoo like taps of little hammers played at his body. Irish's right glove came full into the Italian's ribs. He could feel the rush of air through the Italian's teeth. He brought the hand up with a short chop on the Italian's neck. A scuffle; a semi-wrestle. And again his arms were locked.

"Come on, boys! Come on! Break quick!"

They stood apart, sparred. Irish feinted with the left hand. Feinted with the right. Changed feet quickly, right foot foremost now. Pivoted home with the left hand – Joe Walcott's punch. The Italian side-stepped, and caught him on the ear as he swung to the ropes. Irish turned quickly. A flurry of gloves. Light lead and counter. Clinch.

"You're good, Nick!"

"Y'ain't so bad yourself, Irish."

As the bell finished the round and he walked toward his corner, he was surprised, looking down at himself, to find angry red welts on his body where what he thought was a light tattoo had been beaten. . . .

Yes, he thought between rounds, another little while, another pound of experience, and for all his cunning, his generalship, he could have beaten Nick. And then between him and the championship there would have been only the champion, and the old champion's day was past. He was getting fat, and satisfied, and drinking − and that was bad! And going around the country to Boston and New Orleans and Seattle, beating third-raters and then mainly on points, and lying low, very low indeed, whenever Nick Chip's name was mentioned, or even his, Irish Mike McCann's. Only another six months and he could have taken on the men the champion had beaten: Paul Kennedy of Pittsburgh, and the clever Jewish lad who went by the Irish name of Al Murphy − that fight would have taught him a lot − and the Alabama Kid, the hunched Negro middle-weight who hit like a flail, and Chicago Johnny Kelly − who fought with his right hand first, a hard lad to reach, but he could have beaten him. Could have beaten them all.

He wanted to be champion − knew he could be, with time and experience. And what there was for him in the championship was not personal glory and not money, but a strange pride of race that was hard to explain. All he could do well was this athletic feat of fighting with gloves. There was intuition, a sort of gift. His body balanced right. His left hand moved easily. His right was always in position. All his fights he had won easily. But he had never been up against anyone so good as this Italian veteran.

It seemed to him only right that an Irishman − or an Irish-American, which was better still − should hold the middle-weight and heavy-weight championships. Fighting – clean, hard struggle – was the destiny apportioned to them. He knew enough of the history of his race to remember they had fought under every banner in Europe – the Irish Brigade at Fontenoy, and the men who were in the Pope's Zouaves, and Russia and Germany knew them, and the great regiments the English had, Munsters and Leinsters and Enniskillen Dragoons, and in New York was the beloved Sixty-ninth, the Fighting Sixty-ninth.

Vaguely in his mind there were thoughts which he could not translate into words, it not being his craft, that there was some connection between the men who fought in a padded ring with gloves and the men who went gallantly into battle with two flags above their heads, the flag they served faithfully and the little wisp of green they loved. The men in the ring stood for the men in the field, perhaps. And we should see in the Irish boxer what the cheering ranks of Irish going into battle were. Fight squarely in the ring, fight gallantly, fight to the last drop, and win gallantly and lose gallantly. And let no man say: There is a dirty or mean fighter. And let no man say: There is a coward.

There were Irish names in the ring that made old men's hearts flutter and young men wish they had been born years before. Old John L. Sullivan (God rest the gallant battered bones!) and Tom Sharkey of Dundalk, who never knew when he was beaten, and old Peter Maher, who was somewhere in the house. And there was another name in the mist of past days, the name of a middle-weight champion who had been greatest and most gallant of them all, the elder Jack Dempsey, the Nonpareil. None like him, none! Irish of the Irish, most gallant of them all, he sleeps in a green grave in the West somewhere, and in all men's hearts.

And Irish had thought humbly to fill the Nonpareil's shoes, to fight as hard as he fought, to win as chivalrously, to lose as well, and in his corner as he fought the ghost of the great Nonpareil would be. And the roar of the house as he would walk out at the referee's call, the champion, Irish-American, in his tights of green, and around his waist the starry Western flag.

Ah, well!

The shrill cut of the whistle, and the chief second leaned forward and wiped his face.

"Fift' round, Irish. Keep at him, boy!"

The gong, and the hushed house.

He noticed now that the Italian fighter was no longer resting his left hand semi-casually on his hip, kept up no longer his poise of an Argentine dancer. The Buffalo man's left hand was extended like an iron bar, his shoulder hunched to his jaw for a shield, his head sunk low, as a turtle's head is half-drawn under its carapace; his feet well apart. The man's oily black hair was a tangled mop, and on his ribs were red blotches. His lips were set in a wide line. His black, ophidian eyes snapped and glowed. His poised right hand flickered like a snake's tongue.

And he was punching, punching as hard as he could, hitting squarely with knuckles and every ounce of weight – careless of the economy of the ring that tells a man to save his hands, for a boxer's hands are a boxer's life, and every hurt sinew, every broken knuckle, every jarred delicate bone counts in the long run. The Italian was hitting, hitting like a trip-hammer, hitting for his title.

They faced each other, the Italian poised, drawn like a bowstring, aiming like a sharpshooter, Irish, jigging on his toes, careless of guarding, feinting with the right hand, breaking ground, feinting with the left, feinting with the right again, and then a sudden plunging rush. The jar to his neck as the Italian's straight left caught him flush on the mouth, the whirling crash of infighting, the wrestling clinch. No longer the referee called,

"Break! break!" but tore at them with hysterical hands. A tacit understanding grew between them to protect at all times and as they drew apart they hooked and uppercutted, Irish with an insane mood of fighting, the Italian with quick deliberation: *Snap! Snap!* the punches.

Patter of feet and creak of the boards, and little whine of the ropes. The great blue light overhead, the click of the telegraph instruments below. The running feet of the referee and the nervous patting of his hands, *clop! clop!* The seconds with their eyes glued on the fighting men, and their hands sparring in sympathy. The mooing roar of the crowd and their louder tense silence. And the regular gong, the short respite, hardly a second it seemed, though the interval was a minute – and the gong again.

Once they were so carried away they paid no attention to it, but fought on. Only the referee parted them. Irish held out his glove in apology and they shook hands. The Garden seemed to shake to the cheering.

Whip of lead in the tenth round, crash of counter, deep sock of infighting. Clinch; break. A half-second's inattention on the Italian's part, and the left hand of Irish crashed home to the jaw.

Himself did not understand what had happened until he noticed the crumpled figure on the boards and heard the referee:

"Get back, McCann. Get back!... One!... two...." An immense hysteria of sound filled the house. Men jumped on seats. The telegraph instruments clattered madly. Somewhere near the ring was a fist-fight.

"Three!"

The crumpled figure twitched. At "four" it was dragging itself to its hands. The glazed eyes blinked. Life returned. The Italian shook his head. At "seven" he was on his hands and knees, his head was clearing. At "eight" he was kneeling on one knee, one glove resting on boards. God! how long the seconds were, Irish thought.

"Nine!" Slowly the Italian rose.

The Garden was no longer filled with human beings but with instruments of baritone sound. It hit the roof, rebounded, whirled, surged. All about Irish was sound, sound. In front of him the Italian weak at the knees. The referee hunched like a bowler. Irish jumped in, fists swinging. His fists met crossed arms, elbows, shoulders, but not jaw or head. And suddenly the Italian was clinging to him, as a terrified cat will cling – he couldn't tear himself loose. It took the referee and him to tear the Italian away.

Insane with the din, blind with excitement, he rushed again to meet the beautiful diagonal coverup, left arm across heart and plexus, right crooked about throat and jaw. Again the clinging of the cat. And he felt the Italian growing stronger. It was like a dead man coming to life again. Life was flowing slowly back to shoulders, from shoulders to arms and hands, to hips and knees.

He stood back to consider this miracle, to think what to do next. Two shaking lefts caught him in the face.

And the gong rang and his chance was gone.

Yes another six months and he could have won. He would have known how to keep his head, how to finish the Italian crisply. He had him out, out clean. Another punch would have finished it. And he hadn't experience enough – another six months.

Well, what was the use of grousing! It couldn't be helped. He couldn't pass the fight up when it was offered to him. Right at home, and so much money.

The money had been needed for the home and the old man.

It was funny how much a home cost even on Twenty-fourth Street, and the old man was used to a certain way of living. He liked to have a cook, and a girl to do the work around the house. That was the way it was in Ireland. And the old man needed his decent clothes and his spending money for his little drink and his tobacco and papers, and things like that. He couldn't very well put the old man in lodgings. He wasn't accustomed to that. He wanted his home and the cook and girl. He always was accustomed to it, and why shouldn't he have it?

But a house took an awful lot of money. For what the house cost he and the old man could have stayed at a swell hotel. But the old man liked to be by himself. You couldn't blame him; the old man was entitled to a home. He was a queer, crusty sort, the old man. No harm in him, you know, but just couldn't get on.

And for all that people thought, a boxer's money wasn't easy. A middle-weight didn't get the money light-weights and heavy-weights got. If he'd won the championship – ah, that was all right! Let it go! But when you split fifty-fifty with your manager, there was only half of what you fought for; and there were expenses, too. You had to travel a lot, and be nice to people, too. You had to spend a lot in saloons, though you never drank yourself. Keep your end up with the crowd. And there were always old fighters out of luck, and some of them had families, too. You couldn't refuse them even if you'd wanted to. And who's going to help out a fighter except a fighter? And there was always a lot of poor folks.

It seemed a pity, even for the money end, not to have waited. If he'd waited he'd have had the championship, and then he'd have been fixed for life.

If his old man had been a different kind of old man he'd have gone to him and said: "Hey, old timer, how about going easy on the jack for a while, hey? Just lay off a bit until I get things right.

Gi' me another half-dozen fights under my belt, see, and I'll drop this Guinea cold. And then the champion'll have to give me a fight – the papers'll make him, and you know what he is. He's a bum. So what do you say we get us a couple o' rooms, hey, and go easy for a while? What do you say?"

A different kind of old man would have said: "Sure. We'll take our time, and we'll knock this Guinea for a row of jam-jars. And as for the champion, it's a cinch."

But he wasn't that kind of old man. He didn't hold with this fighting, nohow. He had no use for it. And he wasn't the kind of old guy you could talk to. Irish thought he must have had a hard time in his life.

Ah, well; he was entitled to a good time now. Let him have his own way. Irish could always make money. It didn't matter so much, after all, did it? The only thing that hurt him was that he would never draw the Stars and Stripes through the green Irish tights. . . .

And he could have, if he'd had only six months.

Irish was aware now as he answered the bell that his bolt was shot. The top pitch of concentration had gone. With the dropping of the Italian, and the Italian's escape, he had reached the high point of his fighting, and must now go down. His punch would be heavy still, but it would lack the terrific speed, the speed to shock, that carries a knock-out. And the effect of the cumulation of blows from the Italian sharpshooter was beginning to tell. Through the bruises on his body and neck, and the puffiness of his face, energy was flowing out of him like water from some pierced vessel. The stinging lefts to his face had made it hard for him to breathe, and his hands were swollen inside his gloves, and all of a sudden his legs were tired.

Into ten rounds of whirlwind fighting he had foolishly put

everything, gambled energy and hands and brain.

And he sensed with a great sinking of his heart that Chip was drawing ahead of him now, drawing away from him in the contest, with the inevitableness of the winner drawing away from the beaten man, forging ahead while the other plods hopelessy on. . . . With the quick telepathy of the ring the Italian knew Irish had cracked, that he was gone. And now the energy he had saved by making his man come to him he could use, he must use. For that knock-down in the tenth was a high score of points against him. And he was afraid of a draw. He would have to fight Irish again. Not again! He must knock him out.

He met the futile rushes with stinging lefts. At close quarters he ripped home his hands mercilessly. As they drew apart he stalked his man. *Smack! Smack!* It was no easy matter to avoid the rushing of Irish. God! what a glutton Irish was! What he could take without going down!

Mechanically, stolidly, dully, Irish boxed. All about him now was the hoarse murmur of speculation, and the din of it dazed him a little, and the light. And from a cut in his forehead the blood was running into his eyes.

Four times the gong crashed, the end and opening of a round, and the end and opening of another round. Dully he went to his corner. The splash of water in his face did not revive him, nor the current from the whipping towels, nor the slapping of his legs.

"Don't let him knock you out, Irish. Hold him. Only two more rounds. Don't let him knock you out." Maher's fierce whisper hit at his ear-drums. So it was as bad as that, hey?

"Hold on to him, kid. Don't fight him. Hold him."

The bell rang. They pushed him to his feet. Wearily he moved toward the centre of the ring.

"Look out!" someone called.

The Italian had sprung from his corner with the spring of a cat. And Irish felt surprisedly that he had been struck with two terrific hammers on the jaw. And as he wondered who had hit him his knees buckled surprisingly, and he was on his hands and knees on the floor.

And he heard someone say: "... three ... four ... " He struggled to his feet. Somewhere Maher was shouting. "Take the count, Irish." Irish dully wondered what he meant.

And now Chip was in front of him, concentrated, poised. And once more the hammer crashed on the jaw. And he tumbled to the boards on his side.

He was very dull, very dazed. For a while he knew nothing. And then he understood; the referee pumping his hand up and down, and the roar of the crowd.

"Eight!"

As he moved he felt the ropes, and blindly he groped for them, pulling himself to his feet somehow. About him the din surged. The referee stepped back. The Italian was pawing at the referee's arm, protesting. Irish understood. Chip wanted the fight stopped, didn't want to hit him any more. Ah, he was a good kid, Chip was.

And then the ring slithered underneath him; the hand grasping the rope grew lifeless, let go; and the lights went out for him; and Irish crashed forward on his face.

The old man looked at the battered face above the blue serge suit. "Well," he said, "it must have been a grand fight entirely!"

"It was a great fight," Irish grinned, "and a good man won."

"Meaning yourself?"

"No, meaning the Guinea."

"So you were beat, eh?" the old man jeered. "I never thought you were much good at it."

"Ah, I don't know." And Irish grinned again.

"Tell me," the old man snapped, "did you bring me *The Advocate?*"

"I did." And Irish handed it over.

" 'Tis a wonder you remembered it," the old man snarled. "And the fine lacing you're after taking!"

And Irish grinned again. Wasn't he a queer, grumpy old man!

Padraic Ó Conaire

THE TROUT IN THE BIG RIVER
(translated from the Irish by David Marcus)

I

I WOULD KNOW THAT trout from any other that ever twisted himself in a stream. He has a bulk far greater than most of his relations and the appearance that many of them have not. And the sense of him! The seven parishfuls of fishermen have been troubled and tortured by him for years; every sort of bait that was ever put on a hook, they have tried it – that brazen trout just stretches his pointed snout above the stones where he lives, his tail dancing mockingly, and away with him at his ease.

You would see him under you in the sparkling water, and he not caring a fig for you or your bait however tasty. And wouldn't you just burst with rage to watch him meandering up to the surface and grabbing a little fly the very identical colour and cast as the one on your hook! 'Tis many a curse he wreaked from a fisherman in his time.

Did you tell me you have a wish to go on his trail, my good

Padraic Ó Conaire was born in County Galway in 1883. He gave up a job in the British civil service to travel the roads of Ireland with a donkey and cart and to write only in Irish. The author of a novel, a play and many short stories, there is a statue of him by Albert Power in Eyre Square, Galway. He died in 1928.

trout-fisher? I'll put you right: first, go to Armagh; then, seek out any trout-fisher in that city. Tell him that you heard of The Trout and that you are determined not to leave the place until you have him in your bag.

Oh what a welcome you'll get! You'll be told amazing stories about the fishermen who came from far-off lands to entice The Trout in the Big River. You'll be introduced to every person in the neighbourhood who ever thought of catching The Trout. You'll make pals with the gawky youngster and a firm friendship with the grey old man. Every one of them will show you his fishing-tackle, hook, line, and sinker. He'll give you an account of The Trout, of his girth, of his weight, of his cuteness – ah, I bet you you'll hear stories about The Trout in the Big River that will whack any fishing story in the book. . . .

Sure didn't a young fellow come from Scotland once and take a solemn vow that he would not leave the bank of the river till he'd have The Trout? The poor misguided youth! He did not realize what brains that fish had in his head!

He was there all spring. He had a little log-hut on the bank and food was brought to him every day from the city. The first of summer came. Himself and The Trout got better acquainted. During the long bright summer the man and the fish kept each other company; they even got familiar; until the young man knew what The Trout would do and The Trout knew what the young man would do. . . .

Someone told me that it wasn't fishing the fellow was at all but composing poetry; but who would believe a word from a person who never even put a piece of bait on a hook?

But the place where The Trout lived would draw poetry out of the man who had any strain of it in him at all.

Lustrous water rushing down a slope over shapely green stones. A dark gloomy pool beneath a towering rock. The sur face a lovely mirror for every cloud and bird that scuds across the sky. A bank on each side of it rising smoothly from the water and many-coloured flowers growing there.

And as for the birds round about! 'Tis said that there is not any other place in Ireland where you would see more swallows than beside this pool – hundreds and hundreds sporting and gambolling for themselves over the black water until nightfall.

Amongst the bushes there in the face of summer you would hear the chatter and chirp of every kind of bird! 'Tis there is held the Annual Convention of the Birds of Ireland, and they make as much noise as any other convention: I don't know that there is not as much sense in their noise as well – anyway, if there is not, at least it is sweeter.

II

There's a wood beside the pool. It is wonderful to be in that wood on a bright warm summer's day. There is a hum of bees: a fragrance from every herb, and blade, and tree there. There is a spell there for the man who would be spell-bound.

A pity 'tis not summer there now! A great pity 'tis not summer there now and I in the wood!

I advise the poet to take a trip to that place, to the dark gloomy pool, to the swift lustrous water, to the two flowery banks with their thousands of birds, to the sweet fragrant wood – yes, and to The Trout that reigns over that magic kingdom. . . .

But I never saw The Trout myself with my own two eyes. I never saw the dark pool, or the swift lustrous water, or the wood – except once. But even if I haven't seen them with my own two eyes I have seen them with the eyes of my mind. . . .

Here is how I got to know of The Trout and the pool in the first place:

I'm sitting on my little stool looking dolefully out of the window of a prison-cell at a patch of blue sky, and at the swallows coming between me and that beautiful small patch.

My door opens. A guard walks in.

'Tis evening and he has not much to do. He opens his pocket-book. He takes from it up to twenty baited hooks.

"You're a trout-fisher," says he. "I saw in the office some of the hooks that were in your pocket when you were caught."

I admit I am, that I take somewhat of an interest in trout-fishing. He asks me to name the best fly-bait there ever was. I name it. I praise some baits. I find fault with others. He sees I know about fishing, that I am well skilled in the art.

Then the two trout-fishers get to know each other in a prison-cell.

He had pity for me that I could not make tracks that evening and entice The Trout in the Big River.

He used to come two or three times to my cell every week afterwards, and he used to tell me about The Trout and his adventures, until I well knew that cute fish, the dark gloomy pool where he lived, the two flowery banks, the swift lustrous water, the magic wood beside it. . . .

I would know that trout from any other that ever twisted himself in a stream. And since spring is on the way and the days are stretching, I'll pay a visit to his home. I'll build a little log-hut on the flowery song-drenched bank, and I'll settle down there by myself like the young Scotsman; and sure even if I don't catch The Trout, who knows but perhaps I might stumble on some of the poetry that goes with the place?

John B. Keane

"YOU'RE ON NEXT SUNDAY"

YOU'LL FIND MORE than a few to tell you that there isn't a word of truth in the following story and the nearer you come to the place where it happened you'll find a lot more. When I taxed the man who told me the story with these facts he took his pipe from his mouth, spat into the fire and looked me between the eyes for an embarrassingly long spell. He did not speak but when he returned the pipe to his mouth I knew that the tale was true and that those who belied it were either knaves or fools.

It happened on the fifteenth day of August in the year of our Lord, as they say in these parts, nineteen hundred and thirty-four. It was a fair year for primroses, a better one for hay and a woeful year for funerals.

The Fifteenth as it is still called locally is the annual Pattern Day in the lovely seaside resort of Ballybunion. From all quarters of Kerry, Cork and Limerick would come thousands of country people in every mode of conveyance from bike to omnibus to shanks' mare and pony cart. They still come but in nothing like the vast numbers of yore.

John B. Keane was born in Listowel, County Kerry. He is one of Ireland's most prolific and popular writers. Best known for his plays, he has also published novels, short stories, an autobiography, humorous essays and poetry.

That particular Fifteenth, as I recall, broke fair and clear. Skies were blue. The air was fresh and wholesome and there was a hearty trace of fine breeze from the west. At the creameries and dispensaries that morning man, woman and child wore happy faces.

" 'Tis a great day for the Fifteenth," they would say to each other and back would come the reply, "Ah sure 'tis a great day entirely." At quarter to eleven in the noon of the day my granduncle Morrisheen Digley went forth to the haggard to catch the pony and at the turn of the noon he set forth for Ballybunion in his newly varnished trap. It would do your heart good to see the dancing legs of the pony and the squinting sparks on the flinty road when his iron-shod hooves made light of the long haul. I did not go on the occasion. He said I was too young. Instead he called for his old crony Thady Dowd of Lacca. Neither of the two was under seventy but none gamer set out that day for Ballybunion.

They untackled the pony in the back yard of Mikey Joe's American Bar and celebrated their arrival at the Pattern with two glasses of potstill whiskey. This was followed by a brace of pints, pints of creamy black porter. These were consumed so that the remains of the whiskey might be entirely scoured from the gullet, a most advisable practice this if one is to believe those who are fond of indulging in such procedural drinking.

Towards evening they walked as far as the beach to savour the salt sea air and to partake of a paddle near the shore. According to the old people there was nothing the equal of a paddle in the salt water to cure what might be wrong with you. It was pleasant on the shore. The fresh Atlantic breeze was sharp and bracing but as yet without its late autumnal sting. There were hundreds like themselves pacing up and down, ankle deep in the water, content to dawdle aimlessly until the anxiety for drink returned.

In the village they met neighbours from the townland of Lacca and between them they started a singsong in one of the public houses. When darkness fell a great hunger for meat seized them. They repaired to a café where they were served with succulent steaks and roast potatoes. This was followed by two dishes of rich trifle and the lot was washed down by several cups of strong, well-sugared tea.

"This will make a handy base for more drink," my grand-uncle announced to Thady Dowd. Dowd nodded agreement happily. So far the pair had enjoyed themselves thoroughly and the night was still but a starry-eyed child in swaddling clothes. The best was to come. After the meal they embarked on a grand tour of the village pubs and they had a drink in every single one.

At this stage the reader will begin to raise an eyebrow or two and wonder what is the purpose in the retelling of such a commonplace narrative. Was not their visit to the Pattern but a replica of other years, a common jaunt indulged in by thousands of others and all following the same predictable course?

Patience dear reader and bear with me. As soon as the time came to close the pubs three pairs of well-made civic guards appeared on the street and by their presence ensured that every tavern was cleared. The publicans were grateful enough for theirs had been a long and arduous day. By this stage Thady Dowd and my grand-uncle had more than their share of strong drink but for the purpose of shortening the road home they invested in a half pint of whiskey apiece at Mikey Joe's American Bar.

Earlier they had plied the pony with a sufficiency of oats and when they came to tackle him they found him in excellent fettle. Like all animals who have spent a long day away from the green pastures of home he was full of taspy for the task before him. As soon as he found the open road free from obstacles he started to jogtrot in real earnest. Overhead a full moon lit up the countryside and the sky, its full complement of stars visible in all its quarters, shone like a treasure-house. In the body of the trap the semi-drunken companions sang at the top of their voices to the steady accompaniment of the pony's clopping hooves.

They sang song after song and from time to time they would uncork their whiskey bottles and partake of wholesome slugs. This made them sing all the louder and soon every dog in the countryside was responding. There was an unholy cacophany as the miles fell behind them.

Then, suddenly, for no reason whatsoever the pony stopped in his tracks and despite their most earnest entreaties would not be coaxed into moving a single, solitary inch.

"What's the matter with the creature anyway?" Thady Dowd asked indignantly.

"Beats me," said my grand-uncle. All around there was an unearthly silence save for the chuckling of the Gale River which lay just ahead of them spanned by a narrow bridge. It was the same Gale that poor Spenser the poet did not forget when he wrote about Irish rivers. On the left the crosses and tombstones of Gale Churchyard stood pale and grey in the drenching moonlight. The pony stood rooted to the roadway, head bent, his whole frame taut and tense. There was white foam at the corner of his mouth and a look of abject terror, terrible to behold, in his bloodshot eyes.

"I don't like the look of things," my grand-uncle whispered.

"A rattling damn I don't give," Dowd shouted, "I'm getting out of here to see what the matter is."

"Stay as you are," my grand-uncle counselled but there was no stopping the headstrong Dowd. He jumped on to the roadway and walked round trap and pony several times.

"There's nothing here," he called out. He then proceeded

towards the river thinking that some calamity might have over-
taken the bridge and that the pony, with its animal instinct,
might have sensed this. The bridge was in perfect order. Dowd
looked over its twin parapets into the shallow, warbling water.
He could see nothing unusual.

He retraced his steps and with a scornful toss of his grey head
went towards the graveyard of Gale. As soon as he entered the
little by-road which led to the gateway the pony lifted its head
and followed slowly. It is well to remember that at no time did
my grand-uncle leave the trap. He sat stiffly, holding the reins,
carefully following his friend's every move.

When Dowd leaned across the gate of the graveyard he emitted
a loud yell of genuine surprise. There before him were two hurling teams dressed in togs, jerseys and slippers. Every hurler had
a hurley in his hand and at one side sitting on a low tombstone
sat a small inoffensive-looking, bald-headed man. He wore a white
jersey as distinct from the two teams who wore red and green
respectively. He had a sliotar or hurley ball in one hand and in
the other he held an ancient, burnished, copper hunting horn.

The pony had stopped dead a second time opposite the
gateway over which Dowd was leaning.

"Come away out of that," my grand-uncle called out, "and
leave the dead to themselves."

"What's the use?" Dowd called back, "the pony won't budge
till it suits these people."

"What's the matter?" he called out to the hurlers who stood
about as if they were waiting for something special to happen.
At first no one heeded him but when he called out belligerently
a second time a tall player with a face the colour of limestone
approached the gate. He explained to Dowd that he was the
captain of the red-jerseyed hurlers but that the game could not
start because his team was short a man.

"Who are these teams anyway?" Dowd asked cheekily. The captain explained that his team was Ballyduff and the other team Ballybawn.

"Ho-ho," cried Dowd exultantly. "I'm your man. My mother, God be good to her, was a Ballyduff woman. If you have no objection I will play with your team."

The captain nodded silently and when my grand-uncle called to Dowd to abandon his arrant foolishness the captain turned and addressed him where he sat in the trap.

"Not an inch will you or your pony move," said he in a hollow, haunted voice, "until the final horn is sounded in this game of hurling." My grand-uncle said no more. The pony stood now like a statue and the sounds of the river were no longer to be heard. Overhead the moon shone brightly and the pitch which was the length and breadth of the graveyard, was illuminated as though it were floodlit. Forms appeared from the ground and sat themselves on the graveyard wall. The referee looked upwards at the moon and after a few moments wait blew upon the hunting horn. Then he threw in the ball.

The exchanges started slowly enough with Dowd's team, Ballyduff, getting the worst of it from a faster Ballybawn side. The first score came when the referee awarded a free puck to Ballybawn. He also cautioned a number of the Ballyduff players, notably Dowd and the captain, for abusive language towards himself and for dirty play in general.

The Ballybawn skipper drove the ball straight between the uprights. On the graveyard walls the partisans went wild and a fist fight broke out near the gate. Somebody flung an empty cocoa canister at the referee and he threatened to call off the game if the crowd did not behave themselves. There were a number of fistic exchanges on the field of play but by and large the standard of hurling was as good as my grand-uncle had seen for many a day. There were many fluent movements and excellent long-range scores. The wrist work and pulling left little to be desired. Half time came and went and now the two teams were playing for all they were worth. Time was slipping away and with five minutes to go the sides were level.

Neither would yield an inch. Every player strove manfully to register the single score that would put his own team ahead of the other. The ghostly forms jumped up and down on the walls egging the players on to greater deeds.

It seemed as if the game must end in a draw and the granduncle noted that from time to time the referee looked nervously at the full moon and feverishly fingered his hunting horn, anxious for full time to roll round so that he might wash his hands of the whole affair. There is nothing a referee loves so dearly as a drawn game. The hopes of both sides are kept alive and it is unlikely that he will be assaulted as he leaves the pitch. With less than a minute remaining there was a mêlée at midfield in which Dowd was involved. Fists flew and hurleys were raised. More than once could be heard the clash of ash against doughty skulls.

The referee intervened and taking a scroll from his togs' pocket he commenced the business of taking names. It was during this lull that Dowd sat on a convenient tombstone to savour a richly-merited breather. He withdrew the half pint bottle from his trousers pocket and dolefully surveyed the remnants of his whiskey. The bottle was still quarter full. He raised it to his lips and without once taking it from his head swallowed the contents. Almost immediately he heaved a great sigh which could be heard all over the graveyard. Then he tightened his trousers' belt and waited for play to resume.

With seconds remaining the hunting horn was sounded yet again and the ball was thrown in. Dowd it was who won possession. With a fierce and drunken yell he cut through his opponents like a scythe through switch-grass with the ball poised on the base of his hurley. There were times when he darted like a trout and times when he bounded like a stag. He leaped over gravemounds and skirted crosses and tombstones at breakneck speed. All the time he edged his way nearer the opposing goal line.

Seeing an opening on the left wing he seized his chance and headed straight for the goal with the entire Ballybawn team on his heels like a pack of hungry hounds. Thirty yards out he stopped dead and took a shot. The ball went away to the right but if it did it passed through the eye of a Celtic cross and rebounded off the head of a plaster angel. The rebound was deflected towards the goal by the extended hand of the figure of Michael the Archangel. It skimmed the left upright and found its way to the back of the net. Need I mention that while the ball was travelling so was the empty whiskey bottle which Dowd, with sound foresight, had flung at the Ballybawn goalkeeper as soon as the referee's back was turned. The crowd went wild. The Ballyduff team and supporters milled around Dowd and embraced him. Then they lifted him aloft and trotted round the graveyard on a lap of victory. Finishing the lap the Ballyduff captain called for three cheers for their visitor. Three eerie ullagones went heavenwards and died slowly till the muted river sounds took over once more. The teams had suddenly vanished save for the tall, ghostly presence of the Ballyduff captain. For the first time in over an hour the pony stirred. He pawed the dirt roadway, anxious for the high road.

"Come on at once," my grand-uncle called. Dowd, escorted by the captain, made his way towards the gate where the pony was now prancing and difficult to restrain. Dowd shook hands with the captain and was about to depart when a ghostly hand was laid firmly on his right shoulder. The captain leaned forward and whispered into Dowd's ear. Whatever it was he said Dowd's face underwent a terrible change. The glowing red nose was now puce-coloured and the rosy, whiskey-tinted cheeks were ashen grey. Slowly, almost painfully, he climbed across the gate while the captain faded like a breeze-driven mist behind him.

In the trap Dowd was silent and thoughtful. On his face was a woebegone look that struck a chill in my grand-uncle's heart. The pony highstepped his way homewards, his dark mane flowing loosely behind him, his firm rump bobbing up and down as the miles passed by.

Finally my grand-uncle popped the question.

"What in heaven's name did he say to you?" he asked. Dowd shook his head sadly before he replied. Then he spoke slowly and deliberately with a crack in his voice.

"He informed me," Dowd announced, "that because of the way I played tonight I would be on for good next Sunday."

T.P. O'Mahony

THE BOWLPLAYER

THERE WERE FOUR shots left. Uphill shots over a steep, winding stretch of road with a rough broken surface and a camber that would test the back-axle of any motor car. But there was no motor car in sight. Only the anxious faces of Danno's backers, and the smiles and satisfied grins of those of his opponent.

To hell with all that, thought Danno. Sure there's four shots left and anything can happen. Back there at Mackey's Lane Big Jim had been lucky. A few yards separated the tips, with Danno hind bowl. The next shot was out to a fairly sharp left hand bend, with a muddy grass verge that would swallow up the bowl if the line was wrong. On the other side there was a bank of high grass. And Danno knew that he wouldn't get any lucky rubs from that.

But he played the shot right, stretching the bowl out forty yards. Far enough, and yet not so far as to take all the steam out of it. It broke cleanly and settled into the curve of the bend, running on for a good 110 yards before it stopped and the markers chalked a line on the rough tarmacadam to indicate the tip.

T.P. O'Mahony was born in Cork, where he still lives. He was a leading commentator on religious affairs for the Irish Press *and is now on the staff of the* Cork Examiner. *He has written novels and short stories.*

Danno was pleased with that shot. It was really putting it up to Big Jim. The bastard would have to throw one away — he'd have to. But not this time. Hopping in that grotesque style of his, he spun the cast-iron 28-ounce bowl high into the air in an arc that covered fifty yards of tarmacadam. The line was wrong, and the bowl was speeding towards the grass verge at the apex of the bend. A roar had come from the crowd as they rushed to clear the bend. Danno held his breath, glancing at Big Jim still in a crouched position, the tail of his dirty white shirt flapping in the breeze, and the cap perched peak backwards on the mop of curly black hair.

Suddenly there was another roar, this time of surprise and delight. And Danno knew it came from Big Jim's side. He could hear the babble of voices and the word was passed back. "Got a rub from a brick. Ten yards fore bowl."

Danno's brother, Paddy, looked at him, his face tense and savage. "That bastard is poxed." Big Jim, who was just in front, heard the remark, and turned round pulling on his coat. He grinned, showing yellow broken teeth. "That's bowlplaying." Danno, irritated, rubbed the palm of his right hand down the left hand sleeve of his coat. "Yeah. That's bowlplaying." God, how he knew it. That was bowlplaying all right.

Looking at Danno, one would have seen the smooth unlined face — round and almost baby-like in its freshness — of a man apparently free from even the most common of everyday neuroses. Yet it was the face of a thirty-year-old man who had fathered two children in a marriage which had undergone a progressive deterioration, especially over the last couple of years.

"Here lies a bowlplayer," Danno would often say when he was drunk and had quarrelled with Noreen. Maybe he was thinking in terms of a headstone. But Noreen had other ideas. "Here lies a gambler, a drunkard and a fool," she would reply, standing over him, thin and drawn by work and worry.

Danno could remember the good days. He could remember Noreen, slim and dark and lovely, just the way she was the night they had met at Redbarn in Youghal. New Year's night it was, 1962. Somehow it was like another epoch, the memories of which had almost faded into oblivion. He liked to think that he was a different person then, and that the world was a different place. But he knew it wasn't so. Not really. A man's character is well and truly formed by the time he reaches twenty-one. Wasn't that the case? And the love of bowlplaying, the addiction to it, the eagerness to play, to gamble, perhaps all he had in his pocket, on the strength and skill of his arm, the precision of his eye and the stoutness of his heart — all of these traits were there long before he had met Noreen.

The crowd bustled and hustled around Danno, some of them climbing onto a stone wall just beyond the tips in order to get a better view of the next shot. It was a good crowd for an intermediate championship score. Money was changing hands. Betting on the shots was heavy, even though the sidestake was one hundred and fifteen pounds. Molloy had lost again. Danno should have taken the last shot, he told Paddy. Paddy swore softly under his breath, and then screamed at Dick to go and clear the next bend. "There'll be no bowl thrown here until they open that bend," he said adamantly.

Dick, younger than Danno and Paddy, short and dark, with long fashionable sideburns and a vivid red shirt, was coming back now with a handful of grass. Somebody in the crowd passed a remark and everybody laughed. Even Dick, in spite of himself. It was always like that. Christ, what a bunch. Paddy was pointing. Dick looked out over the outstretched hand. "Do you see that black patch there on the right? Put the sop just at the edge of that. I'll tell you where to drop it. And get those bastards off that bend!"

Dick nodded. "Okay." He hesitated. "What will he do? Do you think he should take it out to that patch?" Paddy, pre-occupied, drew the back of his hand across his mouth. He was thinking how nice a pint would be. But first things first. He was tall and thin, but tough and wiry as a greyhound. "He'll have to. If he drops it he'll get caught in the bushes on the other side. His only chance is to take it away into the track. With a bit of luck he'll make the shore."

Danno was sitting on the wet grassy bank, waiting for the crowd to move out. He held the bowl in his left hand. In his right he held a piece of sharp brown stone, and with this he was tapping the iron, rotating it so as to get a fine coating of powder on it. On a wet day you had to dry and powder your bowl before each shot. That's what they said anyway. And they were right. Danno could remember the mistakes he made in the beginning, the scores that had been lost, thrown away during the early years up Fair Hill and Nash's Boreen and out at Waterloo and the Blackstone Bridge.

And he thought of other mistakes too – mistakes he had made in his courting days with Noreen. He had got drunk often enough trying to blot out the pain of those years. But like a bad dream, it kept coming back.

Faces – anxious, sympathetic, sad – flashed across Danno's field of vision. He could see Paddy hurrying on ahead to assess the situation. A big man in a battered brown hat was waiting for Danno. It was Jack Mullins, one of his regular backers, a man with a relaxed gait and a jovial countenance, but a shrewd judge of bowlplaying talent.

Mullins put a big, meaty arm around Danno's shoulders. "That kind of luck can't last, Danno boy. And the bowl was maggoty anyway." Danno smiled wanly and looked at the big man with the unshaven face. "Maybe, but he's still ahead." "Not to worry. You'll catch him on the hill. But keep shooting those irons. Don't have them near you. The road surface is pretty rough from here to the line." Danno nodded absently. "Hammer the next one, Danno boy," said a voice from behind. "Let yourself go."

Paddy came back from the corner, his lean face drawn and pale. Paddy was a worrier. He came straight to Danno. "Molloy and a few others have switched. They're giving five to four on you. And I haven't seen any takers yet." Danno said nothing. He knew, and he knew that Paddy and Dick knew, that what Molloy and company did made no difference. Not in a score against Big Jim. No, not against that fellow. The only time you knew you had beaten Big Jim was after the final shot had been thrown.

But Danno understood what Paddy was saying, and why he was saying it. And he needed support now, more than Paddy knew.

As usual, a crowd had massed around the tips. The two chalk lines were separated by ten or eleven yards, and the two smooth iron bowls lay on the grass verge. Danno was hind bowl so he would have to throw first. Away ahead of him the road climbed up through a series of sweeping bends, between a wood and on to the finishing line at Burke's Cross. Three shots should do it, unless either or both of the players made a bad mistake.

Three shots. And Danno was depressed by the knowledge that much more depended on those three shots than anyone on the road suspected. He stood on his tip and looked at the grey road ahead. The wood was dark against the horizon, and the overhead clouds looked ominous. Paddy was talking, instructing him. And one of his backers said something about mud. But

Danno didn't hear them. He wasn't listening. He was thinking
of Noreen and of his marriage. Odd how a man gets trapped in
a situation of his own making. But was it really his own doing?
Danno was never sure about these things. He sat on the wet
grass and balanced the smooth iron sphere on his fingertips.
What if the day of reckoning was near? He knew it was. It must
be. And though he cursed bitterly to himself, it was as much at
his own indifference as at anything else. Jesus, how can a man
remake himself? He was what he was, and he had to live with
the consequences. Hadn't he said it a million times?

Paddy was looming over him. "Hey, Danno! Did you hear
what I said?" He looked up at the stern face. "What did you
say?" Paddy squatted down alongside him. "Are you all right?"
he asked, a note of solicitude creeping into his voice. "I'm fine.
Of course I am," said Danno angrily. He pulled himself to his
feet. It was back to square one. "Shove out," he told Paddy.
"And get that crowd off my hand."

The light was failing as the crowd shuffled along the wet road.
Back over Cork City the sky was leaden and heavy. If they didn't
hurry and get on with it, Danno thought fleetingly, they would
catch the rain again. He stood on his tip waiting for the crowd
to split. They would line both sides of the road out beyond the
bend, leaving only Danno's roadshower in the centre with his
legs apart, straddling the imaginary line which the bowl was
intended to follow.

Dick was now forty-five yards from the tip, walking
backwards, watching Paddy's hand. When Paddy waved Dick
dropped the sop, the handful of grass, and flattened it with his
shoe so that the wind wouldn't whip it away. He went on a
further ten yards and then crouched down facing Danno, who
had taken off his coat and given it to Big Jim. Dick glanced
round once more to see that the crowd had cleared the bend.

Then he faced Danno again and added his voice to the cacophony. "Come on, Danno boy! Me life on ye! Put it down for us!"

Danno was walking back behind the tip. Six even paces. He turned and prepared himself for the run-up. He was conscious of the familiar tightness in his stomach, of the expectant hush, the twin lines of faces stretching away before him, and of the green mark forty-five yards away on the grey road.

He was running now and the right hand with its iron missile was sweeping into an arc; he was over the tip and he sprang into the air. For a fraction of a second both feet were clear of the ground and the arc had almost become a circle. The arm was just a blur of speed as it released the bowl. Danno had landed again but the momentum of his run had taken him five yards beyond the tip. All eyes were on the silvery ball of iron. It was a good delivery. Danno had known it even before the bowl hit the road. The direction was right and the cheer told him that it had broken cleanly. But he couldn't see now, for the crowd had spilled out onto the road behind the speeding bowl.

Big Jim was at Danno's shoulder and he handed him his coat. Danno pulled it on as a feeling of relief swept over him. Big Jim lifted the cap and scratched the black mop. "That one went all right," he grunted. Danno smiled thinly. They were at Big Jim's tip. "Yeah. But will it go far enough?" Big Jim laughed and picked up his own bowl. He never gave much away. And if he was worried he certainly didn't show it. They say that he had played Mick Barry once, about ten years ago. He hadn't won, but he had given a good account of himself. And to lose to Barry was no disgrace. He was the greatest, according to the pundits. People called him the Christy Ring of bowlplaying.

Big Jim made no mistake. Steady as a rock, he took full advantage of the eleven yards odds he had. At that particular point in the road they really counted. Shooting his bowl away with power and accuracy, Big Jim managed to increase his lead by another yard or so. Now two shots remained. And the crowd, sensing a close finish, hurried on to the new tips.

Uncertainty began to gnaw at Danno. Big Jim's steadiness unsettled him. He would never crack. And Danno was not helped by the knowledge that the last two shots would have to be played over a stretch of road that was not to his liking. Two years ago he had lost a championship score on this same road, a score that he should have won.

The memory of that mishap was particularly vivid because he had gone off afterwards and got drunk on borrowed money. Somewhere in Shandon Street. And when he got home at two o'clock in the morning, give or take an hour or so, he found that Noreen had locked him out. The bitch. Next day her mood had been vicious, and she had threatened to leave him. So he had repented. And he even managed to keep away from the pubs and the roads for a fortnight. He liked to think that that was because Noreen had said that she hoped he wasn't typical of all bowlplayers. He knew he wasn't, but what the hell. But abstinence didn't last. Perhaps it couldn't. For in a way that he couldn't spell out, Danno had come to accept that bowlplaying was an expression of his real self. On the road, the shallowness of his life semed less real. Chasing that iron ball, there was no pretence, no feelings of inadequacy or frustration or guilt. On the road a man's status was determined by his skill with a 28-ounce ball of cold iron. And Danno was good. At times he was very good. Sure, people sneered at bowlplaying. It was strictly for the proletariat, they said. But what did they know?

Batty finally came back. Danno knew he would. He always came back once during a score. Faithful Batty. Big and bulky, with the familiar faded navy-blue topcoat and the knotted blackthorn stick. They had worked together, courted together, and followed the irons together. Out there on the road, the rapport between Danno and Batty was good, better than that between Danno and his own brothers. When things were going badly, when the shots wouldn't come, the one man whom Danno liked to see, liked to have about, was Batty. God bless him and spare him.

"Well?" Now they were shoulder to shoulder, standing on Danno's tip with two shots to play. "I don't know," said Danno, a little despondently, his eyes fixed straight ahead but not seeing anything. "I'm playing well. I know it. But Big Jim is just shading me all the time. I thought I had him two shots back, but . . ." Batty nodded and scratched his chin. He looked down at his muddy shoes and prodded the wet ground between them with his stick. "It's good bowling. I'd say the two of you are inside the record. Keep it up. Keep the pressure on. You're playing faster than he is, and it'll tell over the last stretch."

Danno seemed unconvinced. Paddy came back and said that he was worried about loose chips on the next bend. Paddy was always worried. Dick said Danno would need plenty of steam with the next one. "Give it plenty of gimp," said Batty in a language which Danno understood. Danno smiled to himself as Batty moved up front again. Gimp, he thought. What a world. Batty looked back at him and waved his stick. "Send us on, old stock. We'll be on the bull's eyes tonight and a back seat in the Col!"

Danno laughed then as he bent to pick up the powdered bowl. Bull's eyes and a back seat in the Col. All in the distant past. The good days. The carefree days. When Danno and Batty would go bowling on a Sunday after Mass. The stakes then were the price of a bag of bull's eyes and a soft seat in the Coliseum Cinema. After all, if you were going to watch Hopalong Cassidy you might as well do it in comfort. Especially if you had won up the road on Sunday morning.

Danno thought of Noreen again. Sometimes you could even buy bull's eyes for two and sit and hold hands in the back seats of the Col. A long time ago. When you were another person. What was the point anyway? The Coliseum was long since closed, and Danno didn't know whether it was still possible to buy bull's eyes. But he could try. Maybe. Maybe if he won, if he beat Big Jim – that bastard – he'd buy a bag of bull's eyes and take them home to Noreen. The trouble was he didn't know whether she'd be there. Oh Christ, the messes I get myself into!

Danno had his coat off, and the cold iron ball in his hand felt heavy. Paddy's anxious face was looking back at him. And out to the corner and beyond the crowd shouted and strained. Danno turned and walked back from the tip. Six even paces. One quick glance to see that nobody was on his hand, and then he started his run-up . . .

Christine Dwyer-Hickey

ACROSS THE EXCELLENT GRASS

A S A CHILD she believed the racecourse was in another country. So different it seemed to her home, just twenty minutes ago. Each suburb passed was a city crossed, each mile a thousand covered. It was as though she had been on a day out with Mary Poppins and button-booted had placed her tiny foot upon a chalk-drawn scene, watching it melt into the pavement as the picture grew to life about her. Losing its flatness and its silence, making her part of a mystery that was not her own.

And this is how small she was then and always walking with the left arm raised and the left hand held by a power greater than hers, that guided and pulled and shrugged her through the crowds and coming face to face with nothing except for handbags square and smooth, or binoculars, badges bunched, swingswong, from their straps. Flutter – "I have been here". Flutter – "I have been there". And no one to see their gold-cut letters save the child that tagged behind.

And then her head would be skimmed by a dealer's stall, sloping downwards and fruit upon fruit laid out in sun-

Christine Dwyer-Hickey was born in Dublin. She won the Powers Gold Label Short Story Award both in 1992 and 1993, and was runner-up in the Observer *short story competition in the latter year. The now defunct Phoenix Park Racecourse is the location of* Across the Excellent Grass.

sharpened cobbles. And it could have been the roof of a Catalan house. And it could have been a Spanish voice that cried in words harsh and unfamiliar "applanorange oranganapple . . . "

And then the arm could come down and wrap itself around her and she would be raised legs loose, little stork, eyes squealing down at the bubbled toes of freshly whitened sandals. Flying yet higher for a moment in a soar so glorious. And then swing and then swoop. And how would they land?

Please not on the bars of the iron-cruel turnstile or not so the dust rises over their straps. Veer to the concrete, clean and hard and the spark that shoots up through the legs won't matter. Just keep the white white, little stork. Keep the white, white.

And then the loud grunt beside her head.

"She's gettin' big, Bill. She's gettin' big."

"Aye, I'll have to be paying for her soon."

Sometimes the crowd, so sure before, would hesitate and stop and the drum of hooves would come from behind the trees, passing in a string so fast they might be caught in a photograph, so fast no individual movement could be seen.

"Quick. What was the first number you saw?"

And quick, she would lisp the first number that came into her head, never really being able to pick out any one in the streak of saddle and flesh and the long bright blur of colour mixed.

"What did she say? What did the child say?"

And for once you could be heard and welcome, face puffed pink from your own importance.

"Ah yes. The luck of the child. Number 3, did she say?"

"What's that in the next race. Ah yes. The child brings him luck."

But he kept a black man in the back of his car for that. Not a full body, just a head and a neck. He said he lost his legs at the Curragh and his hips at Fairyhouse and his arms and his

chest at Cheltenham and he could have lost his willy anywhere.
Longchamps maybe or Ascot. He wouldn't be the first fella to
loose his willy at those places. Now all his luck was in his head
and his brains were in his neck. She said he must have been very
small even when he had all his bits and bobs.

"Ah, but you see," he said, "his mother was a pygmy and his
father was a jockey and it was bound to be so."

And so the head as small as a fist came everywhere, an eye on
either side and cut like a tadpole and being able to see east and
west at the same time. Able to see you no matter which side of
the car you were on. And there were cuts without blood on the
pointed chin and across the mushroom nose where the luck had
chipped off over the years. And she must chip off more and graze
her hands raw if need be, so important it was to the day.

Feeling his hard head on her palm when, after her father, she
would rub her hands in rotation, roundy roundy, and copy the
chant that extracted the luck.

And she was afraid of him. The little black man that was in
charge of the luck.

For yet she might see those elbows sharp above her rise and
move like scissors in the air, and yet she might see fall like con-
fetti to her feet the slow coloured speckles of torn up dockets
drop disappointment on her day.

And she would think of him now, his mean black head stuck
inside the tyre where she had left him, upside down. How angry
he would be. How spiteful if he chose . . .

But the horses pass now and the men in grocers' coats flip back
on either side leaving a gap for the feet to move through. And
the crowd begins to spread itself apart leaving spaces where she
can see now the familiar and the wonderful.

Here on the right and penned in by shining fence, the ring of
careful grass and its outer ring of clay scuffed like brown

meringue, where delicate hooves have tipped themselves upward on parade.

And here, too, another brim with stool after tiny red stool, the exact amount of space from each to each and their spongy seats tight clung with artificial leather.

But not hers now. Not yet. Now a bottom droops loosely over each one. Later on, when spots and flowers and salads of whirling female colour have taken themselves off and later on when the men in straw or donkey brown hats have led the way to celebration or condolences. Then. Then they would be hers, to spin like tops or to teach as her pupils.

And she can watch them from the seat that travels around the tree amongst the green and the quiet and the dots of tickets, thin as tissue and as useless now.

She might eat a bar of chocolate while she waits, square by square and slowly, like on the television. Or the other one, the one that runs in pyramids down a pale yellow tube of paper and foil, the points of chocolate catching on the roof of her mouth at first, them melting softly with almonds and honey and secret crunchings. So long the tube, it may take all year to eat it. So long.

But that would be later on and now is now and her father's thick warm hand is ever pulling.

First walk up to the little house in the middle that looks like a wooden tent. The one whose floorboards moan beneath the feet, and the woman with the white fluffy hair and the chalky lips, penicillin pink. And waiting. Always waiting for the talk to stop.

Up in the air and only some words heard "claiming this and carrying that and ground too this and proved form here and no chance there and Barney Chickle in the long bar says sure fire certainty from the brother's yard and sure fire certainty of losin' if that eejit's tippin' . . . and . . ."

Oh hurry up. Hurry . . . and she grabs the cloth of his trousers, making ding dong bells from the baggy bits behind his knee.

Turns on his heels and nearly knocks her.

"Got to go."

"Good luck."

"Good luck."

Now at last outside and there they are. Up above and skirting the balcony, cloaks red and navy hanging across shoulders and more navy in the hats neat as bricks on top of their heads. And raising instruments like golden toys from the raw knees squeezed up from woollen socks to pursed lips that push and pull sound into shape for the crowd below. And making a change to the mood too and the step; the men a little looser at the knee, the women a little heavier at the hip. And hoop, a flash of brass stands up and caws and here and there a human hums in recognition.

These are the Bold Boys. The boys from Artane. The boys who look no one in the eye unless he, too, wears a cloak and an instrument. Who will come down the wooden steps and march red-necked and eyes down before the "Off", to point their brass to the sky and herald den den derran . . . "The horses are coming, they are coming, here they are."

And it must be easier to go back when the crowds have another spectacle. It must be easiest going back when you can look upwards.

Oh what did they do that was so bold? No one tells. Is it as bold as her bold? Is it as great? Could she end in a place where the devils roam free and sins are kept secret under the fall of a cloak. Could she play music so sweet?

And now turn to the clock standing like a giant's watch with hands so long and spear-tipped pointing at lines. No numbers. Behind it the bushy tails of the Garden Bar peep green through fragile lattice where women move and stop, move and stop, faceless under brims so wide. Except for lips pink and orange and red; one rosebud on each plate.

And more knees stop to greet and more possibilities to be swapped and sometimes stoop and "My, she's getting big" and "That can't be her – I wouldn't know her, so big."

And a child could be a giant before the day is done and a child could wear the watch that is a clock with lines. No numbers. But the child smiles tiny through one eye and dips the other scraping off the trousered-leg she knows . . .

"And do you want to go wee-wee, love?" Mini's rosebud asks and lowers down a hand with fingers knotted and striped with gold, stretching nails she's dipped in blood.

And no one looking down to see her shake her head. No wee-wees.

"Take her, Min', as sure as Jay, she'll want to go in the middle of the race."

So unfair, big fat lie, she never would. She never did. She can go by herself. Big girl.

"See you in the Weigh-Inn then."

"Right so, Min', thanks."

And turns back to Mini's husband, little man, leprechaun face. Used to ride himself before, now he talks his way over every furlong to the winning post.

Min' never says a word when they're alone. Just pulls. The trinkets at her wrist tinkling softly. A fruit basket, a star, a moon, two little balls on a chain. Always talks and buys her crippsanorange, crippsanorange, when daddy's there.

Only one woman in the ladies room looks different. Only one of so many. She wears a coat like a pillowslip with a zip up the front and her hair like a woolly hat pulled around her ears. She is always busy opening doors and handing out pins and eyes looking slyly through the mirror as big brown pennies drop into the ashtray.

They line up by the sinks and all their twins line up in the mirrors and all the while pencils and puffs and brushes touching on this and that on the upturned faces. And silence. Mostly silence. There is nothing to hear but toilets clear their phlegmy throats and tick-tack heels move and stop, move and stop. And "Thank you, Maam, thank you" as the pennies drop.

She hates the smell. The pushy perfume smell. The clouds heavy in the air. It makes her want to vomit. She is afraid she will be too sick for her chocolate. Her eyes sting because of the smell or because she wants to cry. She doen't know which.

Min' comes out, plucking at her skirt. There is blood on her heels where feet, forced into reluctant leather, have been gripped so fiercely that blood has been drawn and cakes between the creases, tough and brown. Min' asks the woman for a plaster. She takes out a foot that is big and mushy and spreads the band-aid onto the wound. Min' doesn't say thank you. Nor does she wash her hands. She puts on more lipstick though and then they leave. Min' doesn't notice that she hasn't done her wee-wees.

They walk into the garden of the gnomes. Her father sits amongst the furrowed faces of the little men. They all stand, feet firm and legs in archways like plastic cowboys. There is no laughter now. Just talk. From earnest mouths that still manage to hang a tipless cigarette from one corner making it dance with words.

Everyone owns dark brown bottles. Some held, some tilted, some left standing for the light to shine through. Her father points his upside down into a glass. He makes black porter rise and leaves a tide of cream loosely on the top. Through his lips he draws black upwards. Ahhh, the tide falls down to the bottom of the glass and clings waiting to be melted.

The little men have funny names. Nipper and Toddy and The Pig. The Pig runs messages for her father, slow winks and wise nods. They pass rolls of money and whisper. Later she will laugh. When her father laughs.

This place makes her think of the city at night when it should be dark, but it is not. The balls of light hanging from the ceiling like street lamps and the crowds that shove at each other, unafraid. Her father stands up. He is as tall as the highest shopfront.

"I'll go up so and take a look at this one."

He fingers through his pocket and takes out a note. He points it at The Pig. "Get a drink for the lads," he says.

The Pig is nodding at each one and asking what he'll have. As seriously as though the money were his own.

And now up the stairs. She pulls herself up the wooden banisters hand over hand. She must stretch her knee up to her shoulder so as not to delay. The man with the loudest voice calls out across the course. Somewhere outside she can hear the Bold Boys denden deren the start.

They walk across the bar and out through the doorway. She can see nothing. Only if she droops her head to where feet stand with feet, down step after step. Or if she leans right back and looks up to the inside-out roof that lets in no sky. She is so small, a flower among the forest.

The man with the voice draws one long word out across the course. It is a word with a thousand syllables screechy and pulled through his nose. The crowd begin to join him, muffling out names of place and colour and unlikely title.

She lifts back her head to look for the bird. She knows he is here somewhere, huge and still, his head turned in profile, his wings spanned over painted flames that rise like feathers from his feet. Then she remembers. He is on the other side of the roof, the bit that slopes like a wooden fringe, where he can see the fences bend and the horses roll slowly across the grass.

The woman on the step below her wears bright red shoes, with heels as long as scarlet pencils. She begins to bounce now, her dress flouncing slightly and her feet clicking up and down again. She stops for a moment, then starts again. This time she lifts one foot altogether from the ground.

There are scratches on the sole of her shoes and a name in gold that is beginning to fade. She recognizes letters that are in her own name and shuffles to the edge of the step to take a closer look. The foot starts to come back to the ground heel first. This time it doesn't return to its own step. This time it reaches in the air and then drops landing on the step above, where her white sandals perch waiting on the edge.

It is like a sword flung from a height onto her toes. She calls out but her voice is silent among the urging and the pleading. "Go on, ye good thing. Go on."

She cannot reach for his leg because her foot is trapped beneath the sword. She is pinned to the step. The tears pop out by themselves and roll like rain down a windscreen. A pain pushes down from her stomach and she screams. She knows what is about to happen. The woman moves her heel away and she is free. But it is too late. She lowers her head, gulping at her sobs. She watches the water trickle down the inside of her legs, down, down, it goes staining the hem of her upturned sock. She opens her legs and lets the rest fall down in little splashes darkening the concrete with its pool.

The roar of the crowd cuts to silence just as the last dribble drops. People begin to reverse themselves and then turn towards her to go back to the bar.

The woman in the red shoes looks at her, then at the pool, then back at her. Her rosebud tightens in disgust.

Afterwards she clutches her chocolate like a staff and walks through the crowds to the green outside. She can hear her father laugh loudly behind her.

"Stay on your tree-seat, I'll be out in ten minutes. Good girl."

She walks on feet she must keep soft and sneaky, laying one before the other as though it were a game. And unheeded by the stragglers and the dealers, she keeps her head down watching the frozen splashes on her sandals and the dent so deep that it is almost a hole. Her thighs smack kisses off each other rubbing the rash that is beginning to rise. Between them she feels her knickers dry hard and crisp, like knives cut into butter.

And in her little head just for a while she forgets her name and this place through which she walks. Though somewhere before her she knows there's a little black man waiting to be unstuck. And behind her the Bold Boys are folding instruments silver and gold into themselves and watching her from a height wade slowly away from the wooden house, across the excellent grass.

Seán O'Faoláin

THE END OF A GOOD MAN

MEN WHO GO into competition with the world are broken into fragments by the world, and it is such men we love to analyse. But men who do not go into competition with the world remain intact, and these men we cannot analyse. They are always contented men, with modest ambitions. Larry Dunne was that kind of man. All that there is to say about him, therefore, is that he bred pigeons and was happy.

And yet, this unconditional lump of reality, this unrefracted thought in the mind of God, suddenly did fall into fragments. He fell for the same reasons as Adam. For when God was saying, "Orchards for Adam," and "Finance for J.P. Morgan," and "Politics for Teddy Roosevelt," and "Pigeons for Larry Dunne," He must have added (*sotto voce*), "But one pigeon he must never control." And it was to that one pigeon, that one ambition, that Larry Dunne gave his heart. The pigeon's name was Brian Boru. Larry got him on his thirty-fifth birthday from his father.

Any evening that summer you could have met Larry at the pigeon club — it sat every night under the canal bridge on the towpath — and you might have guessed in what direction his

Seán O'Faoláin was born in Cork in 1900. His international reputation rests on his mastery of the short story. He also wrote novels, biographies, criticism, travel books, an autobiography and a play. He died in 1991.

heart was already moving by the way he talked endlessly without ever mentioning the fatal bird. You might have heard him, towering over the rest of the club, talking of his runts, tumblers, pouters, homers, racers, without ever mentioning Brian Boru; you might have heard how he had a jacobin, and nearly had a scandaroon; how "pigeons, mind you, must never be washed, only sprayed with rain water. And what's more, pigeons should be sprayed from the shoulders down – never the head, unless you want them to die of meningitis." What a scoundrel the man in Saint Rita's Terrace was, a low fellow who kept budgerigars and had once actually said that pigeons were mere riffraff. How his father had stolen a sacred pigeon out of an Indian temple, when he was in Rangoon with the Royal Irish, and how the rajah chased him into the jungle for two miles trying to catch him. "And what's more, you should never dry a pigeon, unless, to be sure, you wrapped him up in warm flannel – which isn't the same thing." And anyway what were budgerigars, only pups off parrots? "They are not even called budgerigars! They call them budgies – as if anyone would ever dare to call a pigeon a pidgy! Doesn't it show yeh?"

But whatever he spoke of, or whomever he spoke to, you might notice that he never spoke to one little runt of a man who always listened to him with a sly, sneering smile on his face. That was the club member whose Michael Collins the Second had beaten Larry's Brian Boru in every race since the season began – beaten the bird that had laid its beak on Larry's heart.

Nobody knew the history of this Brian Boru. Larry's father swore he was the great-grandson of the Indian rajah's sacred pigeon, but that, of course, was a tall yarn. Whatever its pedigree, the bird was a marvel. Such speed! Such direction! Such a homer! A bird that had only one flaw! Time and again, when there was a race, Larry had seen that faint speck of joy come into the sky over the flat counties and the chequered market gardens where he lived, each time half an hour, at the very least, ahead of every other bird in the team; and on one occasion as much as fifty-eight minutes ahead of them, and that in the teeth of a thirty-mile gale.

For while other birds had to follow the guiding shoreline, or the railway line that dodged the hills, Brian came sailing over mountain-top and moor like an arrow from the bow. Time and again, after greeting him with an adoring shout, Larry had gone tearing back down the lane to his tumble-down cottage, roaring to his da to get out the decoys, and to light the primus stove for some new concoction whose smell was to tempt Brian Boru down to his loft. Back then to the bridge, waving to the sky, calling the bird by name as it came nearer to the parapet on which stood the club's timepiece – a clock with a glass front on which there was a blue-and-green painting of a waterfall. (A bird was not officially home until its owner had tipped the waterfall with its beak.)

But . . . time and again the one flaw told. Brian Boru would circle, and Brian Boru would sink, and inevitably Brian Boru would rise again. After about thirty minutes of this he would come down to the telegraph pole over Larry's back yard, and stay there until some slow coach like Michael Collins the Second had walked off with the race. The bird so loved the air that it could not settle down.

"Oh!" Larry had been heard to moan, as he looked up at the telegraph pole. "Isn't it a sign? Isn't it a symbol? Isn't that poor Ireland all over again? First in the race. Fast as the lightning. But he won't settle down! That bird has too much spirit – he's a highflier – and aren't we the same? Always up in the bloody air. Can't come down to earth." And then he would beseech the bird, as it looked down at him over its prima-donna chest with a bleary eye, rather like an old damp-nosed judge falling asleep on his bench: "Oh Brian Boru! Yeh sweet limb o' the divil, will you come down! Look! I've custards for yeh. I have sowanies for yeh. I have yer loft lined with the sweetest straw." And he would start clucking and chortling at it. "Coordle-coordle-coordle, Brian Boru-u-u-yu." Or: "Tchook, tchuc, thc, thc, thc, thc. Ychook, thc, thc . . . oh, but I'll tchook you if I lay me hands on you, you criminal type from British India! Brian, my *darling*, aren't you *going* to come *down* to me?"

Brian would snuggle his beak on his chest, or make a contemptuous noise like a snore.

Then, that night at the bridge – for on race nights Larry simply had to talk about Brian Boru:

"It's not fair," Larry would protest. "The rules should be altered. That bird is not being given his due. That bird is suffering an injustice. Sure, it's only plain, honest reason. The bird is first home in every race – will any member of the club deny it?"

"No, Larry!" they would reply, appeasingly. "No! He's a grand bird, we all admit it, but a bird who won't settle is no good. And, for another thing, as we're sick and tired of telling you, supposing two birds come into sight at one and the same time, who the blazes is going to tell which one of them is first past the winning post – if there's going to be no winning post?"

"Ah!" Larry would roar. "But sure this bird is home hours before any of your so-called pigeons – cripples, I call them." And then, true to his happy, lighthearted nature, he could not help laughing and making a joke of it. Six feet two, and as innocent as a child. "Did I call them cripples? Cripples is too good for them. The one half of ye must be breeding yeer birds from a cross between penguins and pelicans!"

At which he would recover something of his natural good humour again, and go off chortling – a chortle that would die as he remembered what began it.

As the season approached its end the bird got fat, and Larry got thin; but the bird retained its speed, and Larry became slow-moving and sullen. Those who had always known him for a gay fellow shook their heads sadly over it. He still entered Brian for the races; but each Saturday, now, he would barely stroll to the bridge when the regular two hours were passed since the birds had been released down the country. And when he saw the familiar speck in the sky he would actually turn his back on it.

It was the Easter Monday race that brought things to a head. That day a passing stranger said to him, as Brian Boru came into sight, "Whose bird is that?"

Larry, leaning with his back and two elbows on the parapet, gave an idle glance over his shoulder at the sky.

"Him? He's my bird. But – eh – he's not in the race, you know. He's what you might call a gentleman pigeon. He's doing it for fun. That bird, sir, could win any race he wanted to. But the way it is with him, he couldn't be bothered. Pride is what's wrong with that bird, sir. Pride! Pride, they say, made the angels fall. Maybe it did. I wish something would make that fellow fall."

Whereupon, Larry, as if a new understanding of the nature of pigeons had suddenly been vouchsafed to him, turned and gave the circling speck a terrible look. It was the look of a man struck by rejected love. Just at that moment it was that the man who owned Michael Collins the Second said the fatal word, as they all remembered and often recounted long after. He was a shrimp of a creature, a Tom Thumb of a man, who worked as a boots in a hotel and bred his pigeons out of his tips. Seeing that look of misery in Larry's face he laughed and said, "Why don't you breed budgerigars, Larry? At least you could take them out of their cage and kiss 'em." The row of pigeon fanciers, staring up at the sky, chuckled. They did not see the look of hate in Larry's face, or notice the way he slouched away home to his cabin.

There, as he was at his tea, he suddenly heard the clatter of wings like tearing silk and, looking up through his cabin window, he saw his bird in its loft among the custards and dainties, and now and again it glanced indifferently towards the cabin door. Pushing aside his cup, Larry said to his father – the old man recorded it when there was no use in recording it – "I wish to God, Da, you never gave me that pigeon. That bird isn't human. He despises me." And he put his head between his hands.

Late in the night, while the drizzle of rain fell on him, and the red reflections of the city illuminated the sky, he stood outside until his hair was pricked with the dew of the drizzle, talking now to himself, now to Brian; and though his father kept coming to the door, telling him not to be behaving like a child of two, Larry would not stir. He was like a boy hanging about under the window of his beloved.

"Is it the way you're faulting me?" he whispered. "Is there something you think I ought to do? But what is there I can do? I can't alter the rules, and you won't come down! I know it's a dishonour. It's a dishonour for both of us. I know that, Brian my darling, just as well as you know it. But honest to God, I don't think it's my fault. I brought you up well. I did my best for you. I swear to God above this night I'd lay down my life for you. But, bar flying up in the air myself and bringing you down, what *can* I do?"

From the loft no reply, except the deep breathing of sleep.

Once more he entered the bird. Once more the pigeon scorned the earth. Once more the boots mentioned budgerigars, and this time he added that canaries can at least sing. Once more, Michael Collins won the race. That finished it. Larry went home, and on the following Monday he sold every bird, box, loft, packet of food, and medicine bottle that he possessed. With the money he bought an old Smith and Wesson, thirty-two bore, and five rounds of ammunition from a former pal of the IRA. Then, for the last time, he entered the bird, saw it come, as always, first of the team up against the clouds that floated like bridesmaids over the hedgerows; saw through the veils of the sun how Brian swerved, and circled, and sank . . . and rose again; and did so his usual number of times before making for the inaccessible perch on the telegraph pole. While the dozen heads along the brige shook their commiseration, Larry gripped his revolver in his pocket, and waited for the boots to laugh. The boots laughed. At that Larry's body took on the old fighting slouch; he pulled his hat savagely down over one eye; he buttoned his coat across his chest; he became the old down-looking gunman he had been fifteen years ago when he was in the IRA. Then with a roll of his shoulders like a militiaman, a trick learned from his soldier da, he looked at the boots between the shoulder blades, put on the final bit of the gun-man's manner – the ominously casual strolling gait – and walked quietly down the lane. There he found Brian on the pole.

"Brian," he whispered, but without hope, "will you come down to me now?"

The bird rose and flew away, circled and came back again.

"So yeh won't come down?" whispered Larry out of the corner of his mouth. The bird looked haughtily over the lane roofs, as if contemplating another circle of flight. Before it could stir the shot cracked. With one head-sinking tumble it fell with a plop to the ground. Larry stooped, lifted the hot, twitching body in his palms, gave it one agonized look, and pelted back to the bridge, roaring like a maniac.

"By the Lord Almighty!" they said, when they saw him coming, screeching, with the bird in his palms. "Brian Boru is after winning at last!"

Shouldering their cluster right and left, Larry snapped the beak to the glass of the clock, displayed the celluloid ring on the stiff ankle, and shouted, pale as the clouds, "Has he won?"

It was only then that they saw the blood oozing down between his trembling fingers; but before they could tell him what they thought of him they saw the mad look in his eyes, and the way his hand stole to his pocket.

"Well?" yelled Larry at the boots. "Has he won? Or has he not won? Or maybe you'll say there's a rule that a dead bird can't win a race?"

"He's w-w-won, all right," trembled the boots.

"Gimme his prize!" said Larry.

In fear they gave it to him. It was a new dovecot, painted a lovely green. (*Eau de canal,* the boots called it afterwards, being the sarcastic brute he was.) Larry took the dovecot, and with the reddening beak hanging from his fist he slouched away. On Monday he sold the dovecot, had the bird stuffed and put in the window of his lane cabin for the world to see.

You never see Larry Dunne at the canal bridge now. He walks moodily by himself along the towpaths, idly flickering a little twig against the hedges: or he sits with his father at the other side of the fire, learning off bits from his favourite book, *Who's Who*, or he sits gazing into the dancing devils of flame. The sky outside is lurid with the lights of Dublin. And in the little curtained window, the pigeon looks with two glassy eyes out over the damp market gardens and the heavy, odorous night fields at the bloody sky.

Brian Friel

THE WIDOWHOOD SYSTEM

THE VERY DAY his mother was buried, Harry Quinn set about converting the two attic rooms, from which she had ruled the house for the last nineteen years of her impossible dotage, into a model pigeon loft, so that he could transfer his precious racing birds from the cold, corrugated-iron structure in the back garden. The house, at 16 Distillery Lane, in chaotic condition, already consisted of Harry's ramshackle grocery shop on the ground floor and the flat of Handme Levy, a tailor, on the second. Handme – short for Hand Me Down the Moon (he was six and a half feet tall if he was an inch) – helped with the task of reconstruction, because midwinter was an even slacker time than usual in the tailoring business and because he was already in arrears to Harry, his landlord. Fusilier Lynch gave a hand, too, out of the goodness of his heart. For six days, the three men worked, stopping only to eat the meals that Judith Costigan, who lived next door in No. 15, made for them. When the job was complete, they carried the thirty-six pigeons in, two at a time, each man making six journeys out to the garden, in through the shop, past the smirking tailor's dummies in Handme's living room, and up to the top of the house. Then they

Brian Friel was born in Omagh, County Tyrone. He is one of Ireland's leading playwrights with an international reputation, but his writing career began with two distinguished collections of short stories.

drank in celebration. They drank, as they did after every race, win or lose, in the kitchen behind the shop.

'It's a powerful loft," said Handme. "Height and space and light."

"A castle," murmured the Fusilier.

"You waited one hell of a long time to get them inside, Harry," said Handme. "But it was worth waiting for."

"A palace," said the Fusilier.

Harry suffered from running eyes. They were never dry. Strangers who went into his shop were disturbed by the sight of the weeping shopkeeper. "Now I'm going to tell you something, boys," he announced, mopping his tears with a soiled handkerchief. "Something that's been in my nose for nineteen years."

"You're going to marry Judith!" said Handme.

"I'm going to produce the best racing pigeon Mullaghduff has ever seen. As a matter of fact, boys, I'm going to breed the first local pigeon ever to win the All Ireland Open Championship."

Handme's face was permanently fixed in the expression a man has immediately before he sneezes – mouth open, teeth bared, eyes wide, forehead wrinkled. On him, it became a look of wild delight and anticipation. That on top of a thin, gangling body, made the young girls of the town scared stiff of him. "By God, Harry, you will too!" he cried. "Won't he, Fusilier?"

The Fusilier was short, stocky, silent; he was in his late forties, the youngest of the three bachelors. He was better at greyhounds and whippets than at birds, but a good all-rounder. "How?" he asked cautiously.

"By science," said Harry. "I'll get my bird, train it the way you would train an athlete, feed it right, exercise it right, get to understand its psychology. It's a matter of science."

"By God, you're right, Harry" said Handme. "The All Ireland Open, no less! Eh?"

"And where do you propose getting this wonder bird in the first place?" asked the Fusilier.

Harry paused before he answered. "I'm going to breed it," he said.

"Huh!" The Fusilier laughed drily and began examining his corduroy riding breeches, which were bald at the knees.

"I'm going to breed it scientifically," Harry went on calmly, "according to the theories, principles, and practice of Gregor Johann Mendel."

"Is that the Galway buck that raced the wee grey hen last – ?" Handme began.

"Gregor Johann Mendel says – and in case you boys never heard of him he is a priest and a scientist – he says that a racing pigeon isn't a racing pigeon at all. A racing pigeon, he says, is a bundle of bloody genes. Get the right gene, says he, and you have the winner of the All Ireland cooing in your lap."

"What club is he in, this Mendel fella? Where's his loft?" the Fusilier asked.

"What I've been doing all my life, what every fancier in this country has been doing all their lives," Harry went on softly, "is mating the best cocks with the best hens. Quality with quality, stamina with stamina, speed with speed. And we've all been wasting our time." He leaned across the kitchen table and wiped his eyes so as to get a moment's clear vision of his friends' faces. "According to the Mendelian theory, when you breed champ with champ the offspring generally tends towards the average of the species, unless both members to the union are ..." He faltered. The quotation he had learned from the Pigeon Fanciers Post began to fade. The word "homozygous" pirouetted before his mind and vanished.

"Anyhow," he went on, "the point is this: Quality with quality is no guarantee of quality young ones. Haven't we proved that ourselves? So what I'm going to do now, boys, is the very opposite: fast cock to slow hen, lazy cock to active hen. Until sooner or later I'll have a national winner in my loft. Trial and error – the scientific method. And, by God, boys, with the old woman out of the road and the place to myself, there's nothing to stop me now!"

Later that night, when Harry invited his friends into Judith's house for supper, Handme told her of Harry's scheme. She laughed and said, "Good for you, Harry!" and went on making them a huge feed of rashers and eggs. There never was a more even-tempered, more placid woman than Judith Costigan. When her young scut of a brother, Billy, whom she had reared, sailed for Canada one August morning, leaving her with no means of support except the knitting she did for the glove factory, she laughed and said, "Aren't I lucky to have a roof over my head?" When old Mrs. Quinn became bedridden and summoned Judith to feed and clean her, Judith laughed and said, "It's the least I could do for a neighbour." And on those Saturday nights after a race had been lost or won, when Harry, Handme, and the Fusilier had drunk themselves silly and adjourned to Judith's to round the night off, she laughed most heartily because Harry invariably said to her, "Judith Costigan, someday I'm going to ask you to marry me – someday when I'm good and sober." It was a funny sight to see Harry swaying in the middle of the kitchen floor, his hand on his chest, his cheeks streaming with tears, and Judith, plump, smooth, hazel-eyed, fresher-looking than her forty-four years, nodding her head and laughing generously at him. It was so funny that Handme Levy would forget himself and begin to do a jig, until his spinning head could no longer control his long, miserable shanks and he would fall into a chair and grimace wildly at the ceiling. Then the Fusilier would get maudlin about his time in the British Army – when, as he said, "for four long years my stomach was starved for the whiff of a greyhound." When they had sobered, they would crawl home, and they would not call on Judith again until the next race day, or until they wanted a well-cooked meal.

His mother was not dead a year when the laziest of Harry's hens, which he had paired with a cock with a broken wing, laid two white eggs. The awkward father knocked one of the eggs out of the nest, and it smashed on the concrete floor. Out of the other egg came the bird that Harry was waiting for. Of course he did not know this until he saw it on the wing. But he knew then. Then there was no doubt at all. It was a small pigeon, blue grey, with a white neck and a flat-topped head. Its great pectoral muscle filled its breast and stirred gently against the hand. Its back was broad and strong and straight. Its legs were short. Its full, ovoid body was smothered in velvety feathers.

Handme examined it one Sunday morning. Then he passed it to the Fusilier. Harry waited for their comments. The lofts were open, and the birds, in squadrons of fifteen, flew at the same height as the chapel bells, rolling over the tops of the pines and across the river and out over the barley fields and back to the peaks of the pines again.

"It's a good bird, all right," said Handme. "How does it take off?"

"Clean and straight," said Harry.

"Any trouble in trapping it?"

"None. It lands on the platform and drops right down."

"Aye, it's a good bird, all right," said Handme. "Isn't it. Fusilier?"

The Fusilier handed the bird back to Harry. "It's a cock," he said.

"It's a what?" Handme squealed his surprise.

"I know it's a cock," said Harry with dignity.

"But – but – Harry, you're not thinking of racing a cock, are you?" Handme spluttered. "I mean to say, you never raced a cock in your life – it was always hens. The natural system . . . back to the nest . . ."

"And did I ever do anything worthwhile, racing the natural system?" snapped Harry, suddenly angry. "Isn't that what all the fanciers round here are doing – racing the natural system? A flock of bloody turkeys waddling back to a cosy seat on eggs. And did any man of them ever win a national trophy in his natural life? Well, did they or did they not?"

"Not that I know of," said Handme, subdued more by Harry's voice than by his argument.

"So," said Harry quietly. "I'm going to try the widowhood system. And I'm going to make a job of it."

"You will, too," said Handme. "It's a grand bird, all right."

"Have you mated him yet?" asked the Fusilier.

"Not yet," said Harry. "I'm going to mate him with a wee, fat red hen. I saw him eyeing her."

"Is he keen?" said the Fusilier.

"How the hell would I know? He didn't confide in me!"

"There's nothing wrong with the widowhood system," said the Fusilier calmly, looking out across the still, Sabbatical town, "only for the drawbacks. I seen cocks in my day that were so eager to get back to the hen they battered themselves against the basket and wore themselves out, so that they were too tired to race. And I seen cocks in my day that didn't give a damn if they never saw the hen again. If you want a sure performance, give me a hen every time. A hen will always hurry back to the nest. It's not called the natural system for nothing."

"And what the hell do you think the widowhood system is?" said Harry, wiping his cheeks with the cuff of his jacket. "What could be more natural than for a cock to fly back to its mate?"

"True for you, Harry," Handme agreed, although he was thinking of the young girls of the town scattering in all directions when he met them coming out of the glove factory.

"Anyhow," Harry went on, "I'm sending him to Omagh next Friday week for a tryout the next day. You'll see then if I'm right."

"Thirty miles is too far," said the Fusilier. "Send him to Omagh and that's the last you'll see of him."

"Maybe the Fusilier's right," said Handme. "Why not try Strabane for a first outing? Fifteen miles is plenty for a first outing."

"And you can't race him till he's mated first," said the Fusilier.

"And you're not sure that the red hen'll have him," said Handme.

Harry blinked his eyes and glared from one to the other. "You two," he said, his voice breaking with frustration, "think you know everything! But you know damn all! This is my bird! And I'm going to race him from Omagh! And he'll mate for me! And he'll race for me – scientifically, by the widowhood system!"

He flung open the trapdoor and held the bird on the palms of his hands beneath, as if it were an offering. It spread its wings, hesitated a second, then rose up and out into the spring air, where it joined a squadron of fifteen and tumbled in the waves of the singing bells.

Handme and the Fusilier were right; Omagh was too far. But in everything else they were wrong. On the Tuesday before the race, Harry had paired the bird with the red hen, and she had acquiesced. And on the day before the race, he had held the cock close to the hen until the cock's muscles tensed, but he had not allowed them to breed. Then he slipped the rubber race ring round the pigeon's leg, thrust the bird into the basket, and carried it down to the railway station. The know-all Fusilier was wrong in that detail, too; the bird did not batter itself against the sides of the cage. Indeed, Harry would have been happier if it had shown even some anxiety at being separated from its mate. But it was not an excitable bird, he consoled himself, and surely that is a good thing.

Four other pigeons from the local club were entered for that race, and the best of them, Joe McSorley's checkered hen, clocked in seconds after 11.00 a.m. Major O'Donnell's two birds arrived next at 11.15 a.m. and at 11.18 a.m. At 11.23 a.m. Harry saw Patsy Boyle's ten-year-old hen flit over the pine trees, as fresh as if she were starting out, and she had eight miles farther north to travel. This meant that her velocity was almost as good as the velocity of the Major's birds. Even though all the birds were released from the same place at the same time, each had a different distance to travel back to its own loft, and its speed over its own distance was what mattered. As soon as the birds were liberated, each owner set his timing clock in motion, and as soon as his bird returned he dropped its leg ring into the mechanism and thus stopped the clock. After the race, these clocks were all submitted to the club for examination, and the different times and distances were calculated and the winner determined.

The Angelus bell rang at noon. Harry went up to the loft for the eighth time. His cock had not returned. He boiled potatoes for his lunch and ate them. He washed the counter in the shop, mopped the floor, and disposed of fly-papers that had been hanging from the ceiling since last summer. He climbed the stairs again. Still no bird. Then he threw a handful of maize inside the trapdoor, went down to Handme's bedroom, and shook him awake. "Keep an eye on the shop!" he shouted into the startled eyes. "I'm away out for a pint."

"The bird − is he back?"

"He'll come back in his own good time." said Harry over his shoulder.

His own good time was at six-thirty that evening, and by then Harry and Handme and the Fusilier were sozzled. It was the Fusilier who found him perched in the loft. The two others heard the Fusilier stumbling down the stairs, singing to the bird, "You are my sunshine, my only sunshine. You make me happy when skies are grey".

"Welcome back, wee cock!" cried Handme. "Had you a nice holiday in New York?"

"Don't let me see him!" Harry called, crying into his hands. "He disgusts me – that's what he does, disgusts me."

"Sh-h-h," said the Fusilier. "He's back, isn't he? Isn't that all that matters? Where's the clock? Gimme the timing clock and we'll drop his ring in – just for the record." He kissed the bird gently on the back.

"Take him away!" Harry called. "He disgusts me."

"Hens every time," said Handme. "For reliability and dependability and – "

"Fling him in the loft out of my sight! I still have some bloody pride."

"Now, now, now, boys," said the Fusilier, holding the bird to his cheek.

"He went and had a holiday on top of the Statue of Liberty!" said Handme. "That's what he done!"

"But he'll race!" said Harry. "By God, he'll race before I'm done with him, or I'll know why!"

"He's nothing but a bundle of beans," said Handme, believing he was quoting Gregor Johann Mendel.

"Yes sir, he'll race! I'm not beaten yet, not by a long chalk!"

"You are my sunshine, my only sunshine," sang the Fusilier as he made his way up the stairs again.

That night ended in Judith's house. After she had fed them, she saw Handme's dance and heard the Fusilier's reminiscences about Army life and listened to Harry's tearful proposal. They did not leave her until almost three in the morning, and she was still laughing when she said good night to them.

In the following two months, the bird was raced three times – from Monaghan; from Campbeltown, in Scotland; and from Wexford. Each time, Harry set his timing clock but never submitted it to the local club for scrutiny after the bird had returned. When the other fanciers would ask him was he competing or was he not, he would reply that he was entering but not competing. "I just want him to get some practice," he would say, "but I don't want him to stretch himself until the All Ireland." And they would answer, "Suit yourself, Harry. It's your bird," and wink slyly at one another.

Handme came up with several explanations for the cock's indifferent performances. "I've been studying its skull, Harry," he said, the day after the Monaghan outing. "That's where your trouble lies."

"Aye?"

"It's my opinion, Harry, that the head isn't developed right, with the result that the brain is being squeezed in its cavity."

"Is that your opinion?"

"Doesn't it sound sensible? I think that if we could get some way to develop its skull, there wouldn't be that pressure on its brain. And if its brain wasn't being squeezed, it could concentrate better on flying."

"D'you know what I think, Handme?" Harry replied, with commendable control. "I think that if you stuck to your sewing it might suit all of us a lot better."

After the Campbeltown trial, Handme's explanation was that the pigeon was allergic to salt water. "It's my belief that he was going like a bomb until he was over the North Channel. Then the salt water went for his sinuses and his respiration breathing was done for."

And when the bird took over sixteen hours to return from Wexford on a day that was calm and clear and sunny, Handme said, "Harry, I've got the answer now. He's tired of the wee hen! Give him another hen and you'll find he'll be back before he leaves!"

"He wouldn't be interested in another hen," said Harry.

"He wouldn't what?" said Handme, baring his teeth. "Pigeons are no different to the rest of us!"

"For your information," said Harry, remembering a quotation from the Post, "pigeons tend to be monogamous."

"Is that what Father Mendel says?"

"It is," said Harry wearily.

"You may be sure! That's what's wrong with us in this country – bloody well priest-ridden! And if you ask me, he should know nothing about all that. So take my advice, Harry, and get him another mate."

"It's in him," said Harry, not answering the tailor. "It's deep down in him. All I need is time. Because it's deep down in him."

The Fusilier was of the opinion that the bird was physically perfect but that some delicate imbalance in its psyche caused it to have momentary blackouts when it was on the wing. All birds, he explained to Judith, depended for their direction on the action of the earth's magnetic grid on the membrane of the mind. It had to do with electricity and electrodes, he said. And when Harry's cock was flying it suffered from "mental blackouts, like blown fuses", so that it had to fly blind for periods until the psyche righted itself. Something similar happened to men suffering from shell shock, he believed.

With great peals of laughter, Judith relayed this information to Harry at lunch one Sunday. Ever since his mother had become invalided, he had taken his Sunday meals with her.

"Rubbish!" he said, his tears dropping into the rhubarb pie.

"It sounded great to me," she said.

"All lies," he grunted.

"Well, can you explain how your birds know how to make their way home over hundreds of miles?"

"'Course I can," he said. "It's based on science."

"Science?"

"Every bird has a microscopic eye," he said patiently. "What's the first thing he does when he is liberated? He gets away up into the sky and looks about him. With his two eyes – the kind you and me have – he gets his bearings. But with his microscopic eye – it's buried inside his skull – he sort of takes a photograph of the whole country, like a bloody big map in his head. He knows then exactly where he is and plots his course according."

"Not a doubt in the world?"

"As simple as if he was running on railway lines."

"Lucky bird," said Judith. "Lucky, lucky bird."

For a second, he wondered at the tone of her voice. But almost at once she was laughing again and telling him that she had had a letter from Billy in Canada. He had married, got himself a good job, and wanted her to join him.

"With the microscopic eye," said Harry, "it's as simple as running on railway lines."

The All Ireland Open Championship was held on Saturday, August 5th. All birds had to be at the liberating station, Mizen Head, County Cork, by nine o'clock the night before. They would be released the following morning at ten, weather conditions being clement and propitious, as the Post put it.

Major O'Donnell volunteered to take all the Mullaghduff entrants in his beach wagon to Mizen Head on Friday. There were seven local competitors: Joe McSorley's checkered hen; the Major's two yearlings; Patsy Boyle's old grey hen, her daughter, and her granddaughter; and Harry's cock. The Major sent word to Harry that he would call for the cock after lunch.

That morning, Harry was a mass of nerves. He spilled a bucket of maize on the floor of the loft, and when he was down on his hands and knees, gathering it up, he cracked his head on the handle of the door. The birds sensed his anxiety and flew recklessly from side to side, cooing, colliding, squabbling, injuring themselves. All except the blue-grey cock. He stood quietly beneath the trap, now on one foot, now on the other, blinking his eyes, waiting.

Judith came panting up the stairs. "Harry! Harry, where are you?"

"Up here! In the loft!"

She climbed the remaining stairs. "The Major's below," she gasped, "looking for the basket."

"He's what? Sure, it's not lunchtime yet!"

"It's almost two o'clock," she said. "Come on. Here's the basket. Where's the bird?"

"The bird's not ready. I haven't ringed him yet, and he's not washed, and he has to – "

"Give me," she said, plucking the rubber band from his hand. "This is him, isn't it?"

"That's – Easy! Easy! Handle him gently!"

She picked up the pigeon, turned him over on his back, and slipped the ring over his left foot.

"Now, give him to me," said Harry. "I still have to wash him down."

"You haven't time," she said briskly. "The Major won't wait. Where's the red hen?"

Harry pointed to a nest with a wire-meshed door.

Judith opened the door and put the cock in with the hen. She closed the door again.

The cock spread his wings and arched his neck.

"That's enough,' said Harry. "Take him out."

"Leave them!" she said with quiet authority, as if the loft were hers and not his.

The other birds settled on their perches and went suddenly still.

The hen got to her feet. The cock began beating the mesh with his wings.

"Quick!" Harry snapped. "Before it's too late!"

"Leave them," she said softly, staring at them.

"For God's sake, woman, if you let him go on, he won't come back. He won't race!"

"Leave them," she said again, in a whisper.

"You'll ruin everything! You don't understand – "

"Leave them!"

The hen squatted on the floor. The cock found his balance.

For a second, there was no sound. Then suddenly, violently, Harry pushed her aside. "By God, I won't!" he shouted. He flung open the door and grabbed the cock. The whole loft went mad again.

"You don't understand, woman," he said, thrusting the bird into the basket and talking rapidly to atone for his violence. "If you let him go on, he would never come back. For God's sake, that's the meaning of the widowhood system – to get him to come back. You don't understand these things. They're natural – natural and scientific. Look, he's bustin' to get back to her already! That's what it means, the widowhood system, d'you see?"

"It's a queer system," she said in a dreamy way, still staring into the cage.

"Look at him! Searching for her! Sure, it's the most natural thing in the world. Just because he can't get her. But if you were to leave them together for a week, by God, he wouldn't fly the length of himself to join her! Funny, isn't it?"

"The Major's waiting," she said, turning away from the red hen and going to the top of the stairs.

He lifted the basket and followed her.

The Major took the bird, put it into the back of his beach wagon, and drove off. Harry and she stood together at the edge of the pavement and watched the car disappear round the corner.

"How d'you think it'll do?" he said at last.

She lifted her smooth, round face and looked up at him. "He's bound to come back to her, isn't he?" she asked.

"He'll come back, all right. But it's the time he does it in that matters to me."

"But he'll always come back, looking for her?"

"Naturally!"

"Searching for her?"

"Providing you don't let them mate first — like you were just going to do," he said, laughing.

"I hope you're right, Harry," she said, her hazel eyes looking at something beyond his face.

He sensed her abstraction, a solemnity in her stillness. "Come on inside," he said uneasily, because Judith was strange to him when she was not laughing. "I want you to put a patch on my head."

Together they went into the shop.

The following morning was blue and fragile, but by afternoon the sky became overcast and a drizzle of rain glazed the streets and rooftops. Even if the bird were to do the two hundred and eighty-one miles from Mizen Head in eight hours, Harry calculated – and to beat McSorley's hen it would have to do at least that – it would not arrive back in Mullaghduff until six that evening. But every quarter of an hour after he had made his lunch, he found himself running from the shop to the loft and back again to the shop. Eventually, he closed the shop altogether and joined Handme and the Fusilier in the loft.

He would have been wiser to stay in the shop, because their calm – worse, their assumption that the cock would never make its way back in such weather – unnerved him altogether.

"Ah, well," sighed Handme. "It's a lesson to us all. If he had been a hen, now . . ."

"There's no comparison," said the Fusilier. "Like greyhounds and whippets."

"The wind and the rain might do their damnedest on him," Handme went on, "but he would make it back to the nest, come hell or high water. Nature is a wonderful invention."

"But he's a cock," said the Fusilier.

"And a strong cock, not a bad cock at all, but still a cock," said Handme. The details of the bird's possible loss interested him. "Would he even have made the length of Limerick?" he asked the Fusilier.

"At the very outside," said the Fusilier.

"If the north-Cork hawks didn't get him first."

"Bad brutes, them."

"They've been known to attack children – even north-Cork children."

"Or maybe he broke his neck on the telegraph wires."

"All the same, the spirit would have been game enough."

"He had spirit; I'll say that for him."

"And staying power."

"But a cock," said the Fusilier.

"A good cock, but still a cock."

"Give me the natural system every time."

"That's what's wrong with the widowhood system," said Handme. "It's just not natural."

Harry watched the rain blacken the trunks of the pine trees. "It's in him," he muttered. "It's deep down in him."

"What's that, Harry?" asked the Fusilier.

Harry turned round. "Go in next door," he said, "and tell Judith to make us a pot of tea. We have a couple of hours to wait yet."

"And get us some refreshments when you're out!" Handme called after the Fusilier.

"The All Ireland Open must be a wonderful sight," Handme went on. "To see five or six thousand birds being liberated at the one time." He licked his lips and bared his teeth until the gums showed. "Man, it's something to dream about. A lovely summer morning, and ten thousand fluttering angels rising up to heaven and painting the celestial sky with white and grey and – "

"D'you know what I dream about?" snapped Harry. "That someday you'll pay me the seven months' rent you owe me!"

Handme lowered his head, and Harry went back to the traps and stared out at the rain. Even the birds went silent, squatting motionless on the perches, watching.

The Fusilier came back with two dozen stout and the news that Judith was not at home.

"Of course she's in. She's always in on a Saturday afternoon," said Harry.

"I'm telling you she's not," said the Fusilier. "Go and see for yourself. Anyhow, the gas man's down there, looking to read your meter."

Harry saw to the gas man, and then went into Judith's house. It was empty. He went through the narrow hall, into the kitchen, and out to the back garden, calling, "Judith! Are you home,

Judith?" He stood at the bottom of the stairs and called up, "Judith! Judith?" There was no reply.

Then, for no reason at all except that the race had upset him, the thought suddenly struck him that maybe she was lying dying across the bed. He tore up the stairs and flung open the bedroom door. The room was empty. Only her pink nightdress lay across the bottom of the bed. His calm returned. He came downstairs again, pulled the front door after him, and went back to his own house. Before he went up to the loft, he took a handkerchief from the row that was drying in front of the range in the kitchen, because his eyes were giving him hell.

By the time the bottles were finished, Handme and the Fusilier had discussed politics, the Church, and the decline in public morals. Harry heard them but did not listen. He was battling north with his bird, fighting wind and rain and telegraph poles and hawks. His microscopic eye was not functioning, and he was flying by instinct, doggedly, over wet black bogs and dirty lakes and sodden fields, uncertain if he was going in the right direction but determined to carry on. The terrible effort anaesthetized him; his mind was numb. The labour of keeping his cock aloft and flying and of magnetizing it to himself exhausted him.

"She might," he heard the Fusilier saying.

"It would be the sensible thing to do," said Handme.

Dusk was falling. The birds were making their settling-in, night noises.

"She's still a strong young woman," said Handme.

"And they say Canada's a fine country," said the Fusilier.

"She'll go, all right," said Handme.

Harry dried his eyes. "Go where?" he asked. "Who?"

"I'm just telling the Fusilier here that Judith's thinking of joining the brother in Canada."

"How do you know that?" said Harry. His mind was stirring again. The exhaustion was melting from his body.

"She was telling me herself."

"What about a drink, boys?" the Fusilier broke in. "Do you feel like going out for some, Harry?"

"Yes," said Harry. "Yes – Yes, I'll go and get some."

As he was leaving the loft, Handme was saying, "With all this automation and stuff, what in God's name will men do with their leisure time? That's what worries me."

The smirking dummies in Handme's living room leered at Harry as he passed them, and whispered, "Canada! Canada! Canada!" Their soft, insinuating voices followed him down to the ground floor.

"Like hell!" he said aloud to himself. "Like bloody hell!" But the sound of his own voice, unechoed, unanswered, only aggravated the fear that was growing in him.

Slowly, controlling his steps, refusing to be panicked, he walked into the house next door.

"Judith!" he called sternly. Then again, "Judith!"

When no reply came, his fears babbled to him excitedly. "She's gone! She has packed her bags and is gone! She's gone to Billy in Canada!" He saw her again as she stood in the loft, watching the cock and the hen. He heard her ask, "He'll always come back, looking for her?"

He came out into the street and stood in the rain, and again tried to will his frightened mind into silence. But it would not be still. It drove him into motion, moving his legs, slowly at first, then urging him forward more and more quickly, until he was trotting along Distillery Lane and out the Dublin road towards the glove factory. Of course she was not there. It was the half day; the big iron gates were locked. Nor was she in the church. Nor was she anywhere about the three streets that met in the square. And by now his brain had ceased functioning again, although his body was still fresh – even vigorous. If the mind had been capable of throwing up any suggestion, however absurd – she had gone to visit cousins in Letterkenny; she had gone shopping to Coleraine – he would have gone there at once. But his mind was comatose, and only his stupid body kept going, eagerly, pointlessly. Three times he tried the church; three times he went round the square. And then, exhausted, he came back to her house again.

The door was open. The smell of frying met him in the hall.

"Judith? Judy?"

"Harry?" Her untroubled voice answered from the kitchen.

He closed the door behind him and groped his way through the hall. His tears were blinding him.

From then on, he never knew exactly what happened. Afterwards, he had a vague memory of catching her plump hands in his and kissing them roughly, of her asking him over and over again, "Are you sober, Harry? Are you sober?" and of her laughter bubbling, swelling, rising to an unnatural pitch, and then stopping altogether. He just closed his eyes and held her while she poured out a flow of gibberish about how that afternoon his talk of the widowhood system had given her the idea of going away, going anywhere, with the certainty at first that he would come searching for her. And then, when she was wandering along the Strabane road, how that certainty abandoned her, and how she had had to come back. He knew that he had tried to answer her, but he could only repeat that he had been running in search of her "like a bloody pigeon". He kept saying with incredulity. "Like a bloody stupid pigeon!"

The only memory of their reunion that would always remain sharp and clear to him was of her whispering to him, at some stage, "Will you marry me, Harry?" and of himself kissing her on the mouth in love and gratitude, because somehow, at that moment, the question seemed apt. More than apt – inspired.

It was no time to talk of the race, he was aware of that, but that was what he talked of for the next half hour – of the bird's strength and courage and determination; of his confidence that it would make Mullaghduff, maybe not in winning time, but at least completing the course. (And he was right about that, at least; the cock turned up at the loft just after noon the next day.) Talk of the cock led him to Handme and the Fusilier – the big long string and the wee tight keg – sitting in the dusk of the loft, discussing automation, their feet ringed with empty bottles, waiting for replenishments. The more he talked of them, the funnier they seemed to be. Never before had they seemed funny. After all, they were his friends, his best friends. But now, for the first time, he saw them in another way, and they were ludicrous – two middle-aged men wasting their lives, waiting for a pigeon to come home? He began to chuckle. The chuckle grew into a laugh. In the end, he was laughing so that his sides hurt and his eyes were streaming with water. And in the crook of his arm Judith was laughing, too, and crying, too. And for that half hour, for all the crying, they were the happiest couple in the whole of Mullaghduff.

Somerville and Ross

THE POLICY OF THE CLOSED DOOR

THE DISASTERS AND humiliations that befell me at Drumcurran Fair may yet be remembered. They certainly have not been forgotten in the regions about Skebawn, where the tale of how Bernard Shute and I stole each other's horses has passed into history. The grand-daughter of the Mountain Hare, bought by Mr. Shute with such light-hearted enthusiasm, was restored to that position between the shafts of a cart that she was so well fitted to grace; Moonlighter, his other purchase, spent the two months following on the fair in "favouring" a leg with a strained sinew, and in receiving visits from the local vet, who, however uncertain in his diagnosis of Moonlighter's leg, had accurately estimated the length of Bernard's foot.

Miss Bennett's mare Cruiskeen, alone of the trio, was immediately and thoroughly successful. She went in harness like a hero, she carried Philippa like an elder sister, she was never sick or sorry; as Peter Cadogan summed her up, "That one 'd live

Edith Oenone Somerville was born in 1858 and her cousin, Violet Florence Martin (pseudonym Martin Ross) was born in 1862. Their collaboration began in 1886, and together they wrote a number of novels, of which the most distinguished is The Real Charlotte, *and the celebrated series of short stories about an Irish R.M. (Resident Magistrate). Martin Ross died in 1915 and Dr. Somerville in 1949.*

where another'd die." In her safe keeping Philippa made her debut with hounds at an uneventful morning's cubbing, with no particular result, except that Philippa returned home so stiff that she had to go to bed for a day, and arose more determined than ever to be a fox-hunter.

The opening meet of Mr. Knox's foxhounds was on 1st November, and on that morning Philippa on Cruiskeen, accompanied by me on the Quaker, set out for Ardmeen Cross, the time-honoured fixture for All Saints' Day. The weather was grey and quiet, and full of all the moist sweetness of an Irish autumn. There had been a great deal of rain during the past month; it had turned the bracken to a purple brown, and had filled the hollows with shining splashes of water. The dead leaves were slippery under foot, and the branches above were thinly decked with yellow, where the pallid survivors of summer still clung to their posts. As Philippa and I sedately approached the meet the red coats of Flurry Knox and his whip, Dr. Jerome Hickey, were to be seen on the road at the top of the hill; Cruiskeen put her head in the air, and stared at them with eyes that understood all they portended.

"Sinclair," said my wife hurriedly, as a straggling hound, flogged in by Dr. Hickey, uttered a grievous and melodius howl, "remember, if they find, it's no use to talk to me, for I shan't be able to speak."

I was sufficiently acquainted with Philippa in moments of enthusiasm to exhibit silently the corner of a clean pocket-handkerchief; I have seen her cry when a police constable won a bicycle race in Skebawn; she has wept at hearing Sir Valentine Knox's health drunk with musical honours at a tenants' dinner. It is an amiable custom, but, as she herself admits, it is unbecoming.

An imposing throng, in point of numbers, was gathered at the cross-roads, the riders being almost swamped in the crowd of traps, outside cars, bicyclists, and people on foot. The field was an eminently representative one. The Clan Knox was, as usual, there in force, its more aristocratic members dingily respectable in black coats and tall hats that went impartially to weddings, funerals and hunts, and, like a horse that is past mark of mouth, were no longer to be identified with any special epoch; there was a humbler squireen element in tweeds and flat-brimmed pot-hats, and a good muster of farmers, men of the spare, black-muzzled, West of Ireland type, on horses that ranged from the cart mare, clipped trace high, to shaggy and leggy three-year-olds, none of them hunters, but all of them able to hunt. Philippa and I worked our way to the heart of things, where was Flurry, seated on his brown mare, in what appeared to be a somewhat moody silence. As we exchanged greetings I was aware that his eye was resting with extreme disfavour upon two approaching figures. I put up my eye-glass, and perceived that one of them was Miss Sally Knox, on a tall grey horse; the other was Mr. Bernard Shute, in all the flawless beauty of his first pink coat, mounted on Stockbroker, a well-known, hard-mouthed, big-jumping bay, recently purchased from Dr. Hickey.

During the languors of a damp autumn the neighbourhood had been much nourished and sustained by the privilege of observing and diagnosing the progress of Mr. Shute's flirtation with Miss Sally Knox. What made it all the more enjoyable for the lookers-on – or most of them – was, that although Bernard's courtship was of the nature of a proclamation from the housetops, Miss Knox's attitude left everything to the imagination. To Flurry Knox the romantic but despicable position of slighted rival was comfortably allotted; his sole sympathizers were Philippa and old Mrs. Knox of Aussolas, but no one knew if he needed sympathizers. Flurry was a man of mystery.

Mr. Shute and Miss Knox approached us rapidly, the latter's mount pulling hard.

"Flurry," I said, "isn't that grey the horse Shute bought from you last July at the fair?"

Flurry did not answer me. His face was as black as thunder. He turned his horse round, cursing two country boys who got in his way, with low and concentrated venom, and began to move forward, followed by the hounds. If his wish was to avoid speaking to Miss Sally it was not to be gratified.

"Good morning, Flurry," she began, sitting close down to Moonlighter's ramping jog as she rode up beside her cousin. "What a hurry you're in! We passed no end of people on the road who won't be here for another ten minutes."

"No more will I," was Mr. Knox's cryptic reply, as he spurred the brown mare into a trot.

Moonlighter made a vigorous but frustrated effort to buck, and indemnified himself by a successful kick at a hound.

"Bother you, Flurry! Can't you walk for a minute?" exclaimed Miss Sally, who looked about as large, in relation to her horse, as the conventional tomtit on a round of beef. "You might have more sense than to crack your whip under this horse's nose! I don't believe you know what horse it is even!"

I was not near enough to catch Flurry's reply.

"Well, if you didn't want him to be lent to me you shouldn't have sold him to Mr. Shute!" retorted Miss Knox, in her clear, provoking little voice.

"I suppose he's afraid to ride him himself," said Flurry, turning his horse in at a gate. "Get ahead there, Jerome, can't you? It's better to put them in at this end than to have every one riding on top of them!"

Miss Sally's cheeks were still very pink when I came up and

began to talk to her, and her grey-green eyes had a look in them like those of an angry kitten.

The riders moved slowly down a rough pasture-field, and took up their position along the brow of Ardmeen covert, into which the hounds had already hurled themselves with their customary contempt for the *convenances*. Flurry's hounds, true to their nationality, were in the habit of doing the right thing in the wrong way.

Untouched by autumn, the furze bushes of Ardmeen covert were darkly green, save for a golden fleck of blossom here and there, and the glistening grey cobwebs that stretched from spike to spike. The look of the ordinary gorse covert is familiar to most people as a tidy enclosure of an acre or so, filled with low plants of well-educated gorse; not so many will be found who have experience of it as a rocky, sedgy wilderness, half a mile square, garrisoned with brigades of furze bushes, some of them higher than a horse's head, lean, strong, and cunning, like the foxes that breed in them, impenetrable, with their bristling spikes, as a hedge of bayonets. By dint of infinite leisure and obstinate greed, the cattle had made paths for themselves through the bushes to the patches of grass that they hemmed in; their hoofprints were guides to the explorer, down muddy staircases of rock, and across black intervals of unplumbed bog. The whole covert slanted gradually down to a small river that raced round three sides of it, and beyond the stream, in agreeable contrast, lay a clean and wholesome country of grass fields and banks.

The hounds drew slowly along and down the hill towards the river, and the riders hung about outside the covert, and tried — I can answer for at least one of them — to decide which was the least odious of the ways through it, in the event of the fox breaking at the far side. Miss Sally took up a position not very far from me, and it was easy to see that she had her hands full with her borrowed mount, on whose temper the delay and suspense were visibly telling. His iron-grey neck was white from the chafing of the reins; had the ground under his feet been red-hot he could hardly have sidled and hopped more uncontrollably; nothing but the most impassioned conjugation of the verb to condemn could have supplied any human equivalent for the manner in which he tore holes in the sedgy grass with a furious forefoot. Those who were even superficial judges of character gave his heels a liberal allowance of searoom, and Mr. Shute, who could not be numbered among such, and had, as usual, taken up a position as near Miss Sally as possible, was rewarded by a double knock on his horse's ribs that was a cause of heartless mirth to the lady of his affections.

Not a hound had as yet spoken, but they were forcing their way through the gorse forest and shoving each other jealously aside with growing excitement, and Flurry could be seen at intervals, moving forward in the direction they were indicating. It was at this juncture that the ubiquitous Slipper presented himself at my horse's shoulder.

" 'Tis for the river he's making, Major," he said, with an upward roll of his squinting eyes, that nearly made me sea-sick. "He's a Castle Knox fox that came in this morning, and ye should get ahead down to the ford!"

A tip from Slipper was not to be neglected, and Philippa and I began a cautious progress through the gorse, followed by Miss Knox as quietly as Moonlighter's nerves would permit.

"Wishful has it!" she exclaimed, as a hound came out into view, uttered a sharp yelp, and drove forward.

"Hark! hark!" roared Flurry with at least three r's reverberating in each "hark"; at the same instant came a holloa from the farther side of the river, and Dr. Hickey's renowned and blood-curdling screech was uplifted at the bottom of the covert. Then babel broke forth, as the hounds, converging from every quarter, flung themselves shrieking on the line. Moonlighter went straight up on his hind legs, and dropped again with a bound that sent him crushing past Philippa and Cruiskeen; he did it a second time, and was almost on to the tail of the Quaker, whose bulky person was not to be hurried in any emergency.

"Get on if you can, Major Yeates!" called out Sally, steadying the grey as well as she could in the narrow pathway between the great gorse bushes.

Other horses were thundering behind us, men were shouting to each other in similar passages right and left of us, the cry of the hounds filled the air with a kind of delirium. A low wall with a stick laid along it barred the passage in front of me, and the Quaker firmly and immediately decided not to have it until someone else had dislodged the pole.

"Go ahead!" I shouted, squeezing to one side with heroic disregard of the furze bushes and my new tops.

The words were hardly out of my mouth when Moonlighter, mad with thwarted excitement, shot by me, hurtled over the obstacle with extravagant fury, landed twelve feet beyond it on clattering slippery rock, saved himself from falling with an eel-like forward buck on to sedgy ground, and bolted at full speed down the muddy cattle track. There are corners – rocky, most of them – in that cattle track, that Sally has told me she will remember to her dying day; boggy holes of any depth, ranging between two feet and half-way to Australia, that she says she does not fail to mention in the General Thanksgiving; but at the time they occupied mere fractions of the strenuous seconds in which it was hopeless for her to do anything but try to steer, trust to luck, sit hard down into the saddle and try to stay there.

(For my part, I would as soon try to adhere to the horns of a charging bull as to the crutches of a side-saddle, but happily the necessity is not likely to arise.) I saw Flurry Knox a little ahead of her on the same track, jamming his mare into the furze bushes to get out of her way; he shouted something after her about the ford, and started to gallop for it himself by a breakneck short cut.

The hounds were already across the river, and it was obvious that, ford or no ford, Moonlighter's intentions might be simply expressed in the formula "Be with them I will." It was all downhill to the river, and among the furze bushes and rocks there was neither time nor place to turn him. He rushed at it with a shattering slip upon a streak of rock, with a heavy plunge in the deep ground by the brink; it was as bad a take-off for twenty feet of water as could well be found. The grey horse rose out of the boggy stuff with all the impetus that pace and temper could give, but it was not enough. For one instant the twisting, sliding current was under Sally, the next a veil of water sprang up all round her, and Moonlighter was rolling and lurching in the desperate effort to find foothold in the rocky bed of the stream.

I was following at the best pace I could kick out of the Quaker, and saw the water swirl into her lap as her horse rolled to the near-side. She caught the mane to save herself, but he struggled on to his legs again, and came floundering broadside on to the further bank. In three seconds she had got out of the saddle and flung herself at the bank, grasping the rushes, and trying, in spite of the sodden weight of her habit, to drag herself out of the water.

At the same instant I saw Flurry and the brown mare dashing through the ford, twenty yards higher up. He was off his horse and beside her with that uncanny quickness that Flurry reserved for moments of emergency, and, catching her by the arms, swung her on to the bank as easily as if she had been the kennel terrier.

"Catch the horse!" she called out, scrambling to her feet.

"Damn the horse!" returned Flurry, in the rage that is so often the reaction from a bad scare.

I turned along the bank and made for the ford; by this time it was full of hustling, splashing riders, through whom Bernard Shute, furiously picking up a bad start, drove a devastating way. He tried to turn his horse down the bank towards Miss Knox, but the hounds were running hard, and, to my intense amusement, Stockbroker refused to abandon the chase, and swept his rider away in the wake of his stable companion, Dr. Hickey's young chestnut. By this time two country boys had, as is usual in such cases, risen from the earth, and fished Moonlighter out of the stream. Miss Sally wound up an acrimonious argument with her cousin by observing that she didn't care what he said, and placing her water-logged boot in his obviously unwilling hand, in a second was again in the saddle, gathering up the wet reins with the trembling, clumsy fingers of a person who is thoroughly chilled and in a violent hurry. She set Moonlighter going, and was away in a moment, galloping him at the first fence at a pace that suited his steeple-chasing ideas.

"Mr. Knox!" panted Philippa, who had by this time joined us, "make her go gome!"

"She can go where she likes as far as I'm concerned," responded Mr. Knox, pitching himself on to his mare's back and digging in the spurs.

Moonlighter had already glided over the bank in front of us, with a perfunctory flick at it with his heels; Flurry's mare and Cruiskeen jumped it side by side with equal precision. It was a bank of some five feet high; the Quaker charged it enthusiastically, refused it abruptly, and, according to his infuriating custom at such moments, proceeded to tear hurried mouthfuls of grass.

"Will I give him a couple o' belts, your honour?" shouted one of the running accompaniment of country boys.

"You will!" said I, with some further remarks to the Quaker that I need not commit to paper.

Swish! Whack! The sound was music in my ears, as the good, remorseless ash sapling bent round the Quaker's dappled hind quarters. At the third stripe he launched both his heels in the operator's face; at the fourth he reared undecidedly; at the fifth he bundled over the bank in a manner purged of hesitation.

"Ha!" yelled my assistants, "that'll put the fear o' God in him!" as the Quaker fled headlong after the hunt. "He'll be the betther o' that while he lives!"

Without going quite as far as this, I must admit that for the next half-hour he was astonishingly the better of it.

The Castle Knox fox was making a very pretty line of it over the seven miles that separated him from his home. He headed through a grassy country of Ireland's mild and brilliant green, fenced with sound and buxom banks, enlivened by stone walls, uncompromised by the presence of gates, and yet comfortably laced with lanes for the furtherance of those who had laid to heart Wolsey's valuable advice: "Fling away ambition: by that sin fell the angels." The flotsam and jetsam of the hunt pervaded the landscape: standing on one long bank, three dismounted farmers flogged away at the refusing steeds below them like anglers trying to rise a sulky fish; half a dozen hats, bobbing in a string, showed where the road rider followed the delusive windings of a *bohireen*. It was obvious that in the matter of ambition they would not have caused Cardinal Wolsey a moment's uneasiness; whether angels or otherwise, they were not going to run any risk of falling.

Flurry's red coat was like a beacon, two fields ahead of me, with Philippa following in his tracks; it was the first run worthy of the name that Philippa had ridden, and I blessed Miss Bobby Bennett as I saw Cruiskeen's undefeated fencing. An encouraging twang of the doctor's horn notified that the hounds were giving us a chance; even the Quaker pricked his blunt ears and swerved in his stride to the sound. A stone wall, a rough path of heather, a boggy field, dinted deep and black with hoof marks, and the stern chase was at an end. The hounds had checked on the outskirts of a small wood, and the field, thinned down to a panting dozen or so, viewed us with the disfavour shown by the first flight towards those who unexpectedly add to their select number. In the depths of the wood Dr. Hickey might be heard uttering those singular little yelps of encouragement that to the irreverent suggest a milkman in his dotage. Bernard Shute, who neither knew nor cared what the hounds were doing, was expatiating at great length to an uninterested squireen upon the virtues and perfections of his new mount.

"I did all I knew to come and help you at the river," he said, riding up to the splashed and still dripping Sally, "but Stockbroker wouldn't hear of if. I pulled his ugly head round till his nose was on my boot, but he galloped away just the same!"

"He was quite right," said Miss Sally; "I didn't want you in the least."

As Miss Sally's red gold coil of hair was turned towards me during this speech, I could only infer the glance with which it was delivered, from the fact that Mr. Shute responded to it with one of those firm gazes of adoration in which the neighbourhood took such an interest, and crumbled away into incoherency.

A shout from the top of a hill interrupted the amenities of the check; Flurry was out of the wood in half a dozen seconds, blowing shattering blasts upon his horn, and the hounds rushed to him, knowing the "gone away" note that was never blown in vain. The brown mare came out through the trees and the undergrowth like a woodcock down the wind, and jumped across a stream on to a more than questionable bank; the hounds splashed and struggled after her, and, as they landed, the first ecstatic whimpers broke forth. In a moment it was full cry, discordant, beautiful, and soul-stirring, as the pack spread and sped, and settled to the line. I saw the absurd dazzle of tears in Philippa's eyes, and found time for the insulting proffer of the clean pocket-handkerchief, as we all galloped hard to get away on good terms with the hounds.

It was one of those elect moments in fox-hunting when the fittest alone have survived; even the Quaker's sluggish blood was stirred by good company, and possibly by the remembrance of the singing ash-plant, and he lumbered up tall stone-faced banks and down heavy drops, and across wide ditches, in astounding adherence to the line cut out by Flurry. Cruiskeen went like a book – a story for girls, very pleasant and safe, but rather slow. Moonlighter was pulling Miss Sally on to the sterns of the hounds, flying his banks, rocketing like a pheasant over three-foot walls – committing, in fact, all the crimes induced by youth and over-feeding; he would have done very comfortably with another six or seven stone on his back.

Why Bernard Shute did not come off at every fence and generally die a thousand deaths I cannot explain. Occasionally I rather wished he would, as, from my secure position in the rear, I saw him charging his fences at whatever pace and place seemed good to the thoroughly demoralized Stockbroker, and in so doing cannon heavily against Dr. Hickey on landing over a rotten ditch, jump a wall with his spur rowelling Charlie Knox's boot, and cut in at top speed in front of Flurry, who was scientifically cramming his mare up a very awkward scramble. In so far as I could think of anything beyond Philippa and myself and the next fence, I thought there would be trouble for Mr. Shute in consequence of this last feat. It was a half-hour long to be remembered, in spite of the Quaker's ponderous and unalterable gallop, in spite of the thump with which he came down off his banks, in spite of the confiding manner in which he hung upon my hand.

We were nearing Castle Knox, and the riders began to edge away from the hounds towards a gate that broke the long barrier of the demesne wall. Steaming horses and purple-faced riders clattered and crushed in at the gate; there was a moment of pulling up and listening, in which quivering tails and pumping sides told their own story. Cruiskeen's breathing suggested a cross between a grampus and a gramophone; Philippa's hair had come down, and she had a stitch in her side. Moonlighter, fresher than ever, stamped and dragged at his bit; I thought little Miss Sally looked very white. The bewildering clamour of the hounds was all through the wide laurel plantations. At a word from Flurry, Dr. Hickey shoved his horse ahead and turned down a ride, followed by most of the field.

"Philippa," I said severely, "you've had enough, and you know it."

"Do go up to the house and make them give you something to eat," struck in Miss Sally, twisting Moonlighter round to keep his mind occupied.

"And as for you, Miss Sally," I went on, in the manner of Mr. Fairchild, "the sooner you get off that horse and out of those wet things the better."

Flurry, who was just in front of us, said nothing but gave a short and most disagreeable laugh. Philippa accepted my suggestion with the meekness of exhaustion, but in the circumstances it did not surprise me that Miss Sally did not follow her example.

Then ensued an hour of woodland hunting at its worst and most bewildering. I galloped after Flurry and Miss Sally up and down long glittering lanes of laurel, at every other moment burying my face in the Quaker's coarse white mane to avoid the slash of the branches, and receiving down the back of my neck showers of drops stored up from the rain of the day before; playing an endless game of hide-and-seek with the hounds, and never getting any nearer to them, as they turned and doubled through the thickets of evergreens. Even to my limited understanding of the situation it became clear at length that two foxes were on foot; most of the hounds were hard at work a quarter of a mile away, but Flurry, with a grim face and a faithful three couple, stuck to the failing line of the hunted fox.

There came a moment when Miss Sally and I – who through many vicissitudes had clung to each other – found ourselves at a spot where two rides crossed. Flurry was waiting there, and a little way up one of the rides a couple of hounds were hustling to and fro, with thwarted whimpers half breaking from them; he held up his hand to stop us, and at that identical moment Bernard Shute, like a bolt from the blue, burst upon our vision. It need scarcely be mentioned that he was going at full gallop – I have rarely seen him ride at any other pace – and as he bore down upon Flurry and the hounds, ducking and dodging to avoid the branches, he shouted something about a fox having gone away at the other side of the covert.

"Hold hard!" roared Flurry; "don't you see the hounds, you fool?"

Mr. Shute, to do him justice, held hard with all the strength in his body, but it was of no avail. The bay horse had got his head down and his tail up, there was a piercing yell from a hound as it was ridden over, and Flurry's brown mare will not soon forget the moment when Stockbroker's shoulder took her on the point of the hip and sent her staggering into the laurel branches. As she swung round, Flurry's whip went up, and with a swift backhander the cane and the looped thong caught Bernard across his broad shoulders.

"O Mr. Shute!" shrieked Miss Sally, as I stared dumbfounded; "did that branch hurt you?"

"All right! Nothing to signify!" he called out as he bucketed past, tugging at his horse's head. "Thought someone had hit me at first! Come on, we'll catch 'em up this way!"

He swung perilously into the main ride and was gone, totally unaware of the position that Miss Sally's quickness had saved.

Flurry rode straight up to his cousin, with a pale, dangerous face.

"I suppose you think I'm to stand being ridden over and having my hounds killed to please you," he said; "but you're mistaken. You were very smart, and you may think you've saved him his licking, but you needn't think he won't get it. He'll have it in spite of you, before he goes to his bed this night!"

A man who loses his temper badly because he is badly in love is inevitably ridiculous, far though he may be from thinking himself so. He is also a highly unpleasant person to argue with, and Miss Sally and I held our peace respectfully. He turned his horse and rode away.

Almost instantly the three couple of hounds opened in the underwood near us with a deafening crash, and not twenty yards ahead the hunted fox, dark with wet and mud, slunk across the ride. The hounds were almost on his brush; Moonlighter reared and chafed; the din was redoubled, passed away to a little distance, and suddenly seemed stationary in the middle of the laurels.

"Could he have got into the old ice-house?" exclaimed Miss Sally, with reviving excitement. She pushed ahead, and turned down the narrowest of all the rides that had that day been my portion. At the end of the green tunnel there was a comparatively open space; Flurry's mare was standing in it, riderless, and Flurry himself was hammering with a stone at the padlock of a door that seemed to lead into the heart of a laurel clump. The hounds were baying furiously somewhere back of the entrance, among the laurel stems.

"He's got in by the old ice drain," said Flurry, addressing himself sulkily to me, and ignoring Miss Sally. He had not the least idea of how absurd was his scowling face, draped by the luxuriant hart's-tongues that overhung the doorway.

The padlock yielded, and the opening door revealed a low, dark passage, into which Flurry disappeared, lugging a couple of hounds with him by the scruff of the neck; the remaining two couple bayed implacably at the mouth of the drain. The croak of a rusty bolt told of a second door at the inner end of the passage.

"Look out for the steps, Flurry, they're all broken," called out Miss Sally in tones of honey.

There was no answer. Miss Sally looked at me; her face was serious, but her mischievous eyes made a confederate of me.

"He's in an *awful* rage!" she said. "I'm afraid there will certainly be a row."

A row there certainly was, but it was in the cavern of the ice-house, where the fox had evidently been discovered. Miss Sally suddenly flung Moonlighter's reins to me and slipped off his back.

"Hold him!" she said, and dived into the doorway under the overhanging branches.

Things happened after that with astonishing simultaneousness. There was a shrill exclamation from Miss Sally, the inner door was slammed and bolted, and at one and the same moment the fox darted from the entry, and was away into the wood before one could wink.

"What's happened?" I called out, playing the refractory Moonlighter like a salmon.

Miss Sally appeared at the doorway, looking half scared and half delighted.

"I've bolted him in, and I won't let him out till he promises to be good! I was only just in time to slam the door after the fox bolted out!"

"Great Scott!" I said helplessly.

Miss Sally vanished again into the passage, and the imprisoned hounds continued to express their emotions in the echoing vault of the ice-house. Their master remained mute as the dead, and I trembled.

"Flurry!" I heard Miss Sally say. "Flurry, I – I've locked you in!"

This self-evident piece of information met with no response.

"Shall I tell you why?"

A keener note seemed to indicate that a hound had been kicked.

"I don't care whether you answer me or not, I'm going to tell you!"

There was a pause; apparently telling him was not as simple as had been expected.

"I won't let you out till you promise me something. Ah, Flurry, don't be so cross! What do you say? – Oh, that's a ridiculous thing to say. You know quite well it's not on his account!"

There was another considerable pause.

"Flurry!" said Miss Sally again, in tones that would have wiled a badger from his earth. "Dear Flurry – "

At this point I hurriedly flung Moonlighter's bridle over a branch and withdrew.

My own subsequent adventures are quite immaterial, until the moment when I encountered Miss Sally on the steps of the hall door at Castle Knox.

"I'm just going in to take off these wet things," she said airily.

This was no way to treat a confederate.

"Well?" I said, barring her progress.

"Oh – he – he promised. It's all right," she replied, rather breathlessly.

There was no one about; I waited resolutely for further information. It did not come.

"Did he try to make his own terms?" said I, looking hard at her.

"Yes, he did." She tried to pass me.

"And what did you do?"

"I refused them!" she said, with the sudden stagger of a sob in her voice, as she escaped into the house.

Now what on earth was Sally Knox crying about?

Sam McAughtry

PLAY UP AND PLAY THE GAME

AWAY BACK IN the mid-Thirties, Belfast Corporation laid down a pitch and putt course in the Grove Playing Fields where they ran alongside the Shore Road in North Belfast. Soon after it opened, we were into golf at a mile a minute.

We knew and loved this area anyway. When I was a message boy working for Percy Easton, I used to meet other message boys there, halfway through the morning, behind a hoarding where a hollow lay. It all started with an arrangement between myself and Sanno Whelan, who delivered messages for a butcher on North Queen Street. We would meet behind the hoarding, swap gossip and eat broken biscuits.

In general, grocers tended to look the other way when message boys took the odd handful of broken biscuits as a perk. In normal handling, biscuits broke: all that I did was increase the breakage. I could live with it. Sanno Whelan's contribution was the odd Woodbine that he got for fetching cheap wine from the Gibraltar Bar to an old lady in Spencer Street.

In time, other boys joined us, until on a good morning there would be maybe seven or eight baskets full of goods lying on the grass behind the hoardings and seven or eight message boys

---

Sam McAughtry was born in Belfast. He is one of Northern Ireland's most popular writers and commentators and he also has a wide public among RTE's radio listeners.

comparing notes, eating broken biscuits and passing Woodbines from one to the other. Not all the lads worked for grocers – one delivered for a poultryman and one was a chemist's boy.

When the pitch and putt course was laid down, naturally none of us knew anything about the game, but the idea wasn't hard to grasp. We left our baskets in view, scraped up the tuppence for the hire of one set of clubs – an iron and a putter – tossed for who was to play and away we went around the course.

At first it was just a novelty, good clean fun, as everybody else treated the game. But it wouldn't be Tiger's Bay if the gambling didn't come into it and, sure enough, in a couple of weeks the bets were going down.

It started with broken biscuits, laying odds hole by hole. But the broken ones were mostly digestives and you can go off digestive biscuits after a while. And anyway, the grocers were beginning to ask questions as to how the stiffening seemed to have gone out of their biscuits, all of a sudden. In those days grocers were allowed to hit message boys and lots of them did, certainly Percy Easton thumped me a good few times, and there's only so many blows a lad can take to the head, before the head tells the hands to go a bit easier when they're handling the biscuits. That's when Sanno Whelan saw the chance to make a contribution. We began to bet in sausages as well, these being money for jam for Sanno to knock off out of the butchers.

I was rather good at the pitch and putt.

"Where are you getting all the sausages?" Mother asked.

"There's a flaw in them," I told her. "They're either too fat or too thin and this butcher's very fussy about that, so he gives them to Sanno Whelan his message boy, and he gives them to me."

Times were hard so she didn't pursue the matter, but every now and again I would catch Mother giving me the narrow eye as if to say you're getting away with it this time, but when the economy recovers you're a candidate for a thick ear.

A golfer watching us on what we liked to call the links would have been puzzled to splindereens. For a start, only two were playing but each player had a minder. The minute the ball was struck the striker would take to his heels and run like the clappers after it, and as he flew over the course so a mate of his opponent would run alongside him to where the ball lay.

Now the average golfer would regard this as strange behaviour indeed. The usual routine is to drive off, watch the flight of the ball, shake the head, look pensive, try the stroke again with no ball there any more and then stand back while the opponent does the same. But there was nothing average about us. There wasn't one of us that trusted the other to leave the ball where it landed. We simply weren't made that way.

Our intention in playing pitch and putt wasn't to get the sun, or to kill an idle hour, nor was it to try to overcome the challenge that the course presented. No – our intention was to win broken bisuits or sausages. If a nudge with the foot against the ball helped towards that end, well then, the ball was in for a nudging.

So, for the number of holes that the game lasted, what the watcher would have seen would have been a game that burned up more energy than ice hockey. If the ball were to land out of sight, like in a bit of a dip, then the players and the minders were nothing but a blur. And since even this tight supervision didn't always save the ball from a kicking, it wasn't uncommon to see a fist fight break out, particularly at the dog-leg fourth. With us, golf was a contact sport.

The simple truth of the matter was that there were no sportsmen, as the term is generally understood, amongst us. Certainly the churches tried to argue for fair play, but we just regarded that as yet another near-impossible condition for getting into heaven. We didn't breed good losers. There was no such thing in our book as giving the sucker an even break. Sport, all up and down North Belfast, was run along the same lines as the Massacre at Glencoe.

But we looked after our own, mind. That's why we message boys rallied round when Sanno Whelan was nailed knocking off the sausages, got the sack from his butcher boss, went to join the army as a bugler boy and got turned down because he was too light. Right enough, he looked it. His hips were like two peas in a hanky, he was only five feet and he couldn't have weighed more than six stone. He didn't even do any running at the golf, just watched while the rest of us did.

The army doctor told him to come back when he'd put another half a stone on.

"Funny thing," I said to him, when he came down behind the hoarding to break the news, "you must have carted a mile of sausages here to us for weeks and you weren't eating the things yourself."

"I hate them," he explained, "I hate all meat, after working in the butchers."

He didn't need to go any further. Each one of us hated something. I hate turnips, carrots and parsnips myself. In the house I used to slide them off the plate into my left hand, finish the rest of the dinner, then go upstairs and throw them up the chimney in our front bedroom where the fire was never lit except in time of sickness. To this very day, when I see a waitress or waiter carrying carrots, parsnips or turnips, I feel like scooping them up in my left hand and throwing them up the nearest chimney.

I got Sanno to promise to come down behind the hoarding every working day to keep in touch and he said yes, but he went away very quiet, and the rest of us sat discussing his plight. His father was dead, gassed at the Somme – only lasted five years after the First War. There were brothers and sisters and we could see where he was going to have a problem putting the weight on. We talked about it, remembering that Sanno was quiet, that he felt bad about not being strong enough to run at the golf, that he had given us the only thing he could – his boss's sausages – and we worked out a plan.

Next morning we met as usual, hired out the clubs and started the game. "You've to be my minder," I said to Sanno and my opponent and I took fine care not to run to hard, so that Sanno could keep up. After the time was up, we picked up our baskets and got ready to go.

"Here," I said, handing Sanno half a pound of butter and a packet of good creamy biscuits.

"And take that as well," somebody else said, handing him two soda farls out of a baker's shop.

"And d'ye see these tablets, they're for iron in your blood," said the chemist's boy.

"That's what you call a boiling fowl," the lad from the poultry shop said.

Sanno staggered away under the weight of it all.

"And don't forget to come here tomorrow," we all shouted.

For the next month we carried out the greatest mass knocking-off in history. We knew that we were feeding Sanno's whole family, but there was nothing else for it. They were lean times and his mother was like mine had been with the sausages – she was deferring the enquiry until after the hunger died.

Every day we got Sanno to exercise, running at the golf to watch that there was no skullduggery, or at least that's what he thought he was doing. He got cod liver oil, fresh eggs, the best

of good butter, soda and potato farls, boiling fowl and even bars
of Cadbury chocolate.

It took a month of knocking-off, but we did it. One day Sanno
came to us with a big smile on his face. It was still a farthing
face, but he was weighing in at six stone eight and he was going
for a boy soldier. And they say that crime doesn't pay.

Patrick Campbell

A GOSS ON THE POTTED MEAT

THERE WAS NO doubt that Mr. Jotuni Jaakkala's English was outrageously good.

He seemed to be a lecturer in his native Finnish at Cambridge. "An unhurried existence," as he put it, "seeing that the number of those *in statu pupillari* who wish to study our language and culture is sharply limited by the widespread, but nevertheless groundless, suspicion that we are domiciled in igloos, and live on boiled reindeer's feet."

You could hear the commas tinkling as he shovelled it out.

In the general laughter which followed this ornate revelation, someone, complimenting Mr. Jaakkala on his English, said that he must have lived in England all his life. He looked about thirty.

"I have lived in England since 1947," said Mr. Jaakkala, with charming modesty, "but from the pleasure it has given me you might well say that it has been all my life."

Excited protests followed to the effect that Mr. Jaakkala could

Patrick Campbell was born in Dublin in 1913. He worked for the Irish Times *and spent the war years in the Irish Navy. In 1947 he moved to London, where he became a leading columnist, was described as "the Charlie Chaplin of writing" and blossomed into a highly popular TV personality. In 1963 he became the third Baron Glenavy. He died in 1980.*

not possibly have contrived so perfect an accent, so rich and flexible a vocabulary, in a mere five years.

Mr. Jaakkala smiled with even greater modesty than before, and lit a straight-grain pipe.

I felt compelled to intervene. I didn't like the look of his tweed suit either. For a youthful, *English* don it was exactly right.

"Oh, I don't know," I said, "if you've any ear for music, and it's necessary to learn a language to earn a living, it should be a matter of two or – "

Mr. Jaakkala opened his mouth.

"It should be a matter *only* of two or three years,' I said quickly, "before one becomes entirely fluent."

Mr. Jaakkala smiled again. He knew he'd nearly nipped me. "I believe," he said, "you worked with a German electrical firm in Berlin for some time."

It was a direct invitation to reveal my ear for music.

"Have another glass of sherry before supper?" I said.

Mr. Jaakkala gracefully and confidently declined.

During supper he skimmed up and down and round about the English language with such mastery that gradually everyone else fell silent. To join with him in discussion would have been like accompanying Caruso on a jew's-harp.

After supper it looked as though we might settle down to listen to Mr. Jaakkala for the rest of the night. He had reached Sibelius, and was carving him up with swift, dexterous strokes. I intervened on, "the egregious dramaturgy of the avalanche, translated into terms of the contra-bassoon."

"What about a game of croquet," I said. "Let's go roll those balls."

Mr. Jaakkala, flexible as ever, showed immediate delight.

"Croquet?" he exclaimed. "But indeed yes."

"Don't tell me you play croquet in Finland," I said, surprised.

"Surely the reindeer would get in the way?"

"They do," said Mr. Jaakkala generously. "But not on the immemorial Cambridge sward."

As we walked down to the court, I came to the conclusion that it was even better if he knew something about croquet. The shock, when it came, would be all the greater.

It was decided that I should play with Mr. Jaakkala, against my father, and an elderly economist called Lowther. We seemed to be equally matched, in view of the fact that Lowther, while a fast man with a fiduciary issue, was incapable of getting his back leg out of the way of the mallet, and had never been known to hit the ball more than a few feet.

"It's golf croquet," I told Mr. Jaakkala briefly. "First through the loop wins it for his side, and then all on to the next."

"You mean the hoop?" suggested Mr. Jaakkala.

"No, I don't," I said. I looked at him, puzzled, not getting his meaning. He gripped his mallet uneasily, and looked away. Fractionally, I'd already got him on the run.

"You start," I said, "with the blue. Far side of the loop, coming up."

He played quite a reasonable shot, but hit it too hard. It rolled over the edge of the grass. He stood back.

"Well," I said, after a pause. "The courtesy *remplacement*."

Mr. Jaakkala's brow furrowed. "The put in," my father said. "*Pour la politesse*." I was glad to see that he was abiding by the traditions of the game.

Mr. Jaakkala seemed to get it. He walked after his ball, picked it up, and placed it on the boundary.

As was usual with the first hoop no one succeeded in hitting another ball, and by the end of the first turn we were all lined up at varying intervals along the boundary line. It was Mr. Jaakkala's shot.

I examined the position. "It seems to me," I said, "that after a little Roedeanery off the yellow you should be able to *faire direct pénétration*."

Mr. Jaakkala shaped up to his ball, and then a slight cloud came over his face. "How – " he said – "exactly, do you mean? Could you, perhaps, explain – "

"Explain what?" I asked him.

My father intervened. "He means play a gentle shot off the yellow, which will leave you in posish. Then penetrate the loop."

"Excuse me," said Mr. Jaakkala. "I should like to understand the terms your son has used. This Roedeanery – "

"A lady-like shot off the yellow," I explained. "Followed by position. *Et la loopage*."

Mr. Jaakkala looked at me malevolently. His shoulders hunched. He surveyed the other balls without hope, and suddenly lashed out in the direction of the hoop. He missed it by several feet.

"Which robs," my father said. Mr. Jaakkala walked after his ball, saying something, probably in Finnish, to himself.

Lowther, under my father's direction – two Roedeans, a bumble-over, followed by *pénétration* with a Kurdistan oblique – astonishingly enough made the first hoop, and we all surged down to join Mr. Jaakkala, waiting in silence by the second.

"Well, now," I said, "let's see how she shapes up. We're one down. We don't want to fruddle."

"I do not intend," said Mr. Jaakkala, "to fruddle." He smiled, in a ghastly way. "I presume fruddle to be an onomatopoeic derivative, with the sense of making a mistake."

"It's near enough," I said. "How are you on the Kurdistan oblique?"

"Kindly tell me, please – what is it I am to do?" said Mr. Jaakkala. I knew then that I'd got him, because there, very faintly, like, perhaps, the opening bars of *Finlandia*, was the first sign of the lilting Finnish accent.

"My wife," I said, "born in India, finds it easier to *faire loopage* from an angle of 45 degrees. The Kurdistan oblique. Perhaps we'd better centralise. Take a Roedean on the black."

With the utmost care, Mr. Jaakkala rolled his ball along to hit the black. "Which strikes!" I cried. "Now – stac on the yellow!"

"Pleece?" begged Mr. Jaakkala.

I felt almost sorry for him. "Staccato blow on the yellow," I explained. "It's an in case."

Mr. Jaakkala peered about him like a man who'd lost his glasses.

"*Fair removage* of the yellow!" I cried, urging him on, "in case you fail on *pénétration* of the loop!"

I let him get his mallet about half-way back when I flung my own on the ground in front of him. I shouted, "STOP!" Mr. Jaakkala started convulsively and then shot me a glance in which fear and rebellion were mixed in equal parts.

"Total change of plan!" I cried. "Do a goss on the potted meat!"

This time it was Mr Jaakkala who flung his mallet on the ground. "Aie goss!" he cried wildly. "How do I know what is aie goss – ?"

Lowther intervened. He probably thought that violence was going to be done. "A gossamer, or glancing blow," he said hurriedly – "on the potted meat."

"Vaat iss potted mitt?" roared Mr. Jaakkala.

Lowther seemed stunned. We'd been calling it the potted meat so long that he was incapable of providing a translation.

"The red," said my father.

"The paint's coming off it," I explained. "It looks like potted meat. Chicken and ham."

"Awwwh!" said Mr. Jaakkala. It was a kind of groan. He took a pace back, and then with a low, sideways sweep he flogged out at the blue. It struck the yellow about half-way up, and crushed it into the jaws of the hoop. The blue ball sped on and disappeared, at the height of several feet, through the back netting.

"That's done it," I said. "You've gone and played an onomatopoeic derivative."

"The total fruddle," my father said.

"You've gone and yawssed the jellow ball."

"What? Pleece? I do not know – ?" Mr. Jaakkala was miles out at sea.

"You've jawsed the yellow," I said. "A former Swedish Consul in Dublin, a regular player here, always referred to it as a yawssing of the jellow. His accent," I added, "was not impeccable."

"I yawss the jellow," said Jaakkala wonderingly. "I yawss the jellow." He tried it again. "Is it good, yes?" He was like a small child with a new toy.

I clapped him bravely on the back. "It's a beezer, boy," I said. "*Faire remplacement!* Take your goss on the potted meat!"

He did as he was told. He finished up with as fine a Kurdistan bouncer as we had ever seen, the blue ball leaping over the jellow in the yawss, to *faire* a tremendous *loopage*.

After the game, which we won easily, was over, Mr. Jaakkala drank a pint of whiskey with echoing cries of "Skoal!" Before he left he delivered an address in Finnish, and then had to be helped down the steps.

I only hope he pulled himself together before his lectures began again next term.

Dermot Somers

CLIFF HANGER

E VERY WARM SUNDAY crowds visit the car parks at Glendalough for the brooding scenery and monastic ruins. Tourists stroll the paths and lounge in leafy sunlight, separated from the landscape like an audience at an epic film. There is a cinematic sense of composed history and posed geology about the place now. Imaginary monks and saints queue up at the ice-cream vans and Portaloos.

But the blind eye of the Upper Lake records time accurately – with the static truth of a mirror. Time is in the still background, the mute immobile skyline. Life flits across the glass, like an insect, without impinging at all on the deep reflection.

Not everybody stays within umbilical reach of the car park. A mile beyond the lake, high above the narrow floor of the valley, there is a line of steep, grey cliffs. The granite glistens when the mica-flecks unite to reflect the benevolence of the sun. Every crack, every slab, every corner up there on the remote skyline has a name and grade, a detailed topography of hand and foot-holds. On any warm weekend tiny climbers can be seen strung out below the rocky horizon like gaudy scraps of bunting.

Dermot Somers was born in County Roscommon. He has written extensively on mountaineering and was a member of the Irish team which successfully climbed Everest in 1993. He has published two collections of short stories which have been widely acclaimed.

One deep, blue Sunday a college club milled about at the foot of those cliffs, sweating faces, strident mouths, parched throats from the gruelling slog up the long boulder-scree. There was a multi-coloured medley of ropes and climbing gear to be divided out among the novices. An air of hilarious incompetence prevailed, perplexed persons stepping carefully into harnesses like bondage-straps, people posing nervous questions about bowline knots and figure-eights, while a few of the more expert – some self-appointed – went about supervising the preparations, and especially paying intimate attention to the tying of girls' knots.

Mick Dowling had a special technique of demonstrating a bowline which involved brushing his knuckles across the victim's thighs and then in a low curve over the abdomen as he tied the rope. Mick belonged to that familiar breed of clubmen who lick their lips in lascivious unison ever year when the novices troop innocently into the fold. The girls are creamed off by the fellowship and scrutinised, not for enthusiasm or talent, but for their response to the charms of macho-mountaineers. The ceremony is a fertility ritual for the kind of men who hang around climbing clubs as a substitute for more immediate modes of masculinity.

Dowling certainly looked the part though – burly, broad-shouldered, with a square-cut rugged face, and an affectation of headbands and tight tracksuits. But if you took power-weight ratio into account he was considerably more meat than muscle, and would never make a dexterous climber. And if you knew a little bit about crags and mountains, it was obvious his experience didn't add up to much either; but shy first-year students didn't know the Index from the Eiger and were wildly impressed when he showed snow-shrouded slides or waved to them from a rock-climb in Dalkey Quarry.

The only other third-year climber in the club was Vincent Barry, a silent youth with an intense and inward air. He kept an awkward distance from the club and its bantering intimacies.

Vincent was beginning to climb solo in the Quarry this year, lurching doggedly unroped from one familiar handhold to the next on the impersonal granite that questioned nothing but his nerve. He was obsessed with the suspense and surprise of climbing, the excitement of placing his body in an apparently implausible position, and extracting it safely upwards, with what he hoped was polished skill. But there was very little elegance in his diffident persistence, slouching silently on long legs in baggy clothing. He was often pointed out to new members with a kind of derisory pride as the club's Odd Man Out, the exception that emphasised the happy unity of the rest.

What Vincent needed was a determined climbing-partner, someone to challenge him, the kind of relationship where he would fight his way up a hard climb, knowing that if he didn't do it his partner would.

There were several of those teams on the general scene and Vincent envied their confidence and commitment. They did new routes, free-climbing old aid-moves, chattered in pubs about handjams and overhangs, miming moves in the air with an extravagant semaphore.

Ideally he should have climbed with Mick Dowling for their mutual improvement, but their natures were antagonistic. Vincent had no interest in Mick's extrovert style which involved nonchalant repeats of climbs he already knew well, where the leader's protection was as good as a safety-net.

Today at Glendalough Vincent was preparing to take a couple of beginners up Quartz Gully, a fine climb of middling difficulty. They were strong and fit, and he saw no reason why they shouldn't be capable of the grade. He distrusted the tradition that kept beginners on easy climbs until they developed an awed resistance to difficulty. His nerves bristled when Mick approached with a superficial air of brotherly concern.

"What route are you bringing the lads up, Vinny? Have they done the easy slab yet?"

"I don't now whether they have or not. We're doing Quartz Gully." Vincent's answer was sharp. He knew Mick was the sort who felt his own expert status was threatened by beginners who showed a lot of promise.

"Are you sure that's wise? Do you reckon they're up to Quartz?"

"They'll be fine," Vincent snapped. His judgement was being undermined in front of the group listening nervously to the exchange. Mick shrugged easily and turned back to his own charge, capture-of-the-season Janette Stirling, a striking, fairhaired girl who looked about seventeen until her cool voice and sharp, mature eyes cut deep into the observer's giddy pretension. She was twenty-two years old, had worked in Manchester for four years before coming back to Dublin to study.

On a few evening meets in Dalkey Quarry with the club Janette had shown a smooth command of technical rock, although she had no inclination to lead. Technically the climbing is the same whether the rope is above one or below, but the leader requires commitment and the ability to place protection.

"I climbed a lot when I lived in Manchester," she told her wide-eyed admirers in dismissal of her ability. "We . . . I . . . used to go to the Peak District every weekend," she added. Her listeners recognised romance behind that "we" chopped off with a quick frown.

Vincent had been very excited by her self-contained poise as she followed his lead up the intimidating headwall of In Absentia but he could only nod and smile tightly in response to her thanks at the top. Then, as Mick appeared effusively on the path behind them, he turned abruptly away to untie the rope.

Mick had stood on the ground below while Vincent led the exposed climb. He shouted up instructions to Janette about the moves and the holds, managing to demonstrate his familiarity with the hard climb without having to risk leading it in front of her. Vincent raged silently as they walked back down the steps into the Quarry, Janette smiling affectionately at Mick who was sketching lavish moves in the air.

"I'll take you up a few good climbs in Glendalough . . ." Mick's gloating voice had churned up through the intimate dusk.

Eventually all the novices at the crag were teamed up with leaders. Some had already gobbled all their supplies, condemning themselves recklessly to a day of drought. The majority were doing the short routes at the base of the buttress, a popular group exercise with scope for ribaldry and relaxation.

It looked as if no one was ever going to ask, so Mick announced to a sudden hush that he was taking Janette up . . . Prelude and Nightmare. He put a kind of ghoulish emphasis on Nightmare. Even those who had never heard of the famous and excellent climb winding its protracted line up the full height of the main face were struck with the dizzy romance of suspense.

Vincent thought grimly that this would be at least Mick's seventy-seventh ascent of the route: he should be able to climb it blindfolded, and it was all big holds anyway; for all its impressive steepness the climbing was mostly straightforward, and even the hardest section at the start of the Nightmare pitch was overrated. There was a lot of nonsense talked about Nightmare, Vincent thought, but it started on a big, flat ledge, even if it was two hundred feet above the ground. And that old piton in the short crack above the ledge somehow gave people a sense of peril. But modern protection and ropework were so good that the furthest you could fall at that point was about six feet. Fair enough, it was a different story in the old days, but people were still cultivating myths and legends just to invest the bit of ultra-safe rockclimbing they did with an aura of adventure.

He could imagine how Mick would milk the occasion for all it was worth, casually stamping his own image on the vertical landscape – "... that's Spillikin over there, the overhanging ridge. It's the hardest climb in Wicklow ..." – contriving the impression that he'd be off climbing routes like Spillikin himself if he wasn't nobly engaged in conducting Janette up routes he could climb with boxing-gloves on.

Vincent was seething with frustration as he eased his charges up their climb with a discreetly tight rope. He desperately wanted to try Sarcophagus, one of the great test-pieces of the crag, unmatched for quality anywhere in the country they said, even on the mighty cliffs of Fair Head. The line looked awesomely impossible. Boldly direct up the mainface, and then into a clean, pure corner flaunting its architecture high overhead like a crease in a church-steeple. From below it seemed to overhang in blind rejection of human aspiration, and yet there was a thin crack in the back of that corner, handholds and footholds on the walls, and there would even be faint traces of black rubber where hundreds of feet had tip-toed towards what Vincent thought must surely be immortality.

He would have to ask Mick to climb it with him. No one else could. Mick hadn't done Sarcophagus either, but he wasn't likely to try it today. He wouldn't risk failing before an audience.

A breathless choking in his throat muffled the hope that Janette might offer to follow him instead.

After a couple of hours he descended to the festive base. Anyone who had a lunch was enjoying it under the envious supervision of those who hadn't. Mick and Janette were the centre of attention. Vincent couldn't understand how anyone with a voice so measured and a gaze so self-contained could allow herself to be the focus of that circus.

"Well, I reckon we've set up a record today, Vinny," Mick greeted him with grinning self-satisfaction. "Prelude and Nightmare in forty-seven minutes flat. We were really movin', man!"

"Great suff," Vincent responded absently. "Listen, Mick . . ." He dropped earnestly on one knee beside the lolling figure. "What about Sarcophagus? Since you're going so well . . ." he flattered. "Do you think we could give it a lash after lunch?"

He paused ungently, but his face – unused to expression – looked wooden.

"Sorry Vincent. I'm going up with Janette to do Aisling."

"I suppose you're going to time that as well," Vincent rasped, jerking to his feet in disappointed fury.

"Well now, Vinny," Mick said indulgently, "you have to admit three-quarters of an hour isn't bad for Prelude and Nightmare. I can't see you doing better."

He was teasing. No one would bother to time a rock-climb, but it amused him to see Vincent so het-up.

"I'll halve it!" snarled Vincent blindly.

"That'll be some trick!' Mick laughed, sitting up. "How will you manage that?"

"Solo!"

"Don't be silly . . ." Janette's scornful voice rang through the babble of exclamations as Vincent hurled away, stumbling ignominiously on the steep ground.

He rushed along the heathery base of the crag, sick with fury and fear as the challenge swelled from a defiant stab within him to a nauseous enormity churning in his stomach. His head tipped back and he stared up the relentless wall reeling above him.

Where did it go ... did he even know where it went ... ? His eyes raked the blurring crag without recognition. Yells and running steps behind him, Mick's mates to the fore, the rest of the mob trailing.

Looking away for deliverance his fevered vision raced down the boulder-field to the cool, enamelled lake and the distant track by the shore vanishing into the woods away from this sickening mistake. He jerked his attention back to the brutal crag, and the track still hung in his eye with the diminishing dot of his own figure running along the edge of the lake.

Where was the start of the bloody route ... a ramp, wasn't it? He had climbed it two years before, on the safe end of a rope. The ramp balance, awkward, leading to a hard scrabbling pull up a steep slab. People sometimes hurtled twenty feet from those moves back down to the sloping ground ... And off to hospital, his mind exaggerated ludicrously.

He was standing under it now, the rock utterly inorganic, shining with slick heat. Looking up he saw ledges gashing the face from side to side, reassuring in their promise of roots and rests. But the bald, bulging rock between them ...

The anxious spectators – a lynch mob, he thought – were almost on his heels, but he felt entirely alone. Through the panting and irrelevant babble of voices he heard the hostile thud of his own heart; each beat had the crisp overtone of a shell under stress, a kind of brittle tick.

There was a bird piercing the air with a shrill needle of song, another scraping its beak feverishly against a glass sky; and all around them, enclosing the voices, heartbeat, bird-sound, there was the waiting calm of a windy place on a still day.

His hands floated limply towards the rock, like rubber fists in a nightmare boxing match. Before pulling into the first move he swiped in panic at the sole of each foot to dry off any grass-sap or cuckoo-spit that might undermine friction.

He hauled up on flaky incut holds, his fingers digging with unnecessary pain into the crisp rock, until his body was level with the narrow, tilted ledge of the ramp. As he edged an agoniseding toe out onto its polished surface, his body tense, teeth clenched, fingers pinching the rock, he heard the first brazen shout.

"Ten seconds!" the voices yelled in clamorous unison.

The first beat of the blood-chant it seemed to him. His body stalled in mid-move. Heat rushed to his face and hands. Sweat beaded. Light flared on the rock, there was a buzzing in his brain. Bluebottles swarming round the Lord of the Flies. Paralysed by the impression, he couldn't move, a skinny body hanging on awkward rock glaring its fear.

"Fifteen seconds, sixteen seconds, seventeen seconds . . ."

Mick's loud voice penetrated his paranoia, an anxious entreaty. "Will you come down out of that, Vinny, and don't be acting the eejit!"

And then he was moving again, traversing the diagonal ramp cravenly, toes shuffling on its outer edge, fingers clinging to the crease where it met the face, then a side-pull higher and he lurched out left onto a long foothold. He lay trembling against the short, steep wall that separated him from the ledges above. Stretching up to his full height he fumbled at the flat handholds, his fingers and forearms straining to lift the body that was making no more effort than a carcase to assist in its own elevation.

The thought of lifting his feet off the secure foothold and running his toes on friction up to the exposed rock was unbearable. With his stomach curved in against the wall he strained helplessly, his fingers futile. Space gnawed at his ankles, and he shot a glance down at the narrow foothold for reassurance.

"One minute!" the chant brazened.

He had to lean out from the rock to get his feet up, but as his body arched the strain increased on his fingers. His toes kicked onto the gritty, holdless rock. On sweating fingertips he pulled viciously, shuffling his feet up, shifting his weight on to implausible friction, and flung one hand high to a better hold, greasy skin welding itself to the coarse granite.

Heaving his body higher – while his imagination failed and hurtled horribly down the rock – he was pressing down now on the handholds in a mantelshelf move, right leg coming up inch by inch and scraping onto a foothold.

There was an audible release of tension below, a concerted sigh of relief which reached Vincent's strained perception as a menacing hiss.

"Two minutes thirty seconds," piped a lone voice, a beginner, callous with innocence.

The first hard moves were over and Vincent felt utterly drained. If he found that so hard, what chance had he higher up, on Nightmare? He was drained of tension as well. He knew he was safe; he was going to give up.

If he could have traversed off at that point he would, but the logical escape was a little higher, just before the start of Nightmare. He could scramble aside and descend a gully then.

Mechanically he ascended easy ledges towards the next problem. He was being funnelled upwards into a steep inverted V in the cliff. He stood fifty feet above the ground, enclosed like a small statue in the rocky niche. His white shirt shone in the pocket of shadow. There was a piton in a mossy crack, the old-fashioned protection for the escape move out left. He imagined the slender, nylon rope around his waist, clipped securely into that piton, and paid out from behind by a firmly anchored second.

He recalled a steep, blind move here, pivoting on a poor foothold with a hidden grip to swing around the edge of the niche. But there were handholds like gloves to reach after the first move. Get it over with! A moment of delicate blance, a fingery pull, and he had the good hold, fingers curled over the lip and then slotted into the knuckles.

A wall of clean rock hung steeply above him with a sense of friability where it had been scuffed bare of vegetation. It was split by a good, rough crack. Strenuous to start, he fixed his eye on a high handhold and launched himself vertically upwards, heart thudding, as the grudging holds multiplied.

A chorus of diminished voices announced the four-minute mark. They knew he would descend the gully.

He thought of athletes skimming over flat ground, a four-minute mile, five thousand two hundred and eighty feet. In four minutes he had dragged himself one hundred and fifty feet upwards, on his fingertips, to a narrow ledge with a gigantic flake of granite rearing behind it.

The absurdity of the comparison squeezed an hysterical giggle out of him. Four minutes and he was near the top of Prelude already. He could make the halfway mark in six or seven. At that rate he could finish the double-route in a quarter of an hour and make a total mockery of Mick. Why, a good climber – and he had no illusions about himself on that score – could probably do Prelude and Nightmare in less than eight minutes solo!

His brain swam deliriously as mental arithmetic took over from exposure and fear. Again he looked out and saw the sandy track by the lake-shore vanishing into the cool seclusion of the trees. This time he saw himself, not running away, but triumphant on the path. Victory bubbled in him. Another ten minutes could make him a hero. Not much of a hero, he understood.

There were plenty of people who soloed incredibly hard climbs, and they didn't necessarily amount to much either. But heroism was all about who you needed to impress.

He didn't hear the five-minute call, if it was uttered at all, for he was working up the groove behind the huge flake. He reached the top of Prelude and its intersection with the escape-route.

A pair of traditional stalwarts making their way up the gully stared in alarm at the pale spectre emerging from the top of Prelude, its eyes set with belligerent intensity, face and hair slick with sweat.

"What's all the shouting about?" they demanded, with the nervousness of men who suspect that every crisis is bound to involve them. Wordlessly the apparition in baggy trousers and soaking shirt shook its head and disappeared out rightwards to Nightmare Ledge.

Depending on a climber's confidence this flat platform in the middle of the very steep wall is a small or a large ledge, combining an insecure or a safe stance with a superb or an intimidating sense of exposure. Resolutely Vincent faced the crucial crack. His legs tightened and trembled as the short, fierce-looking problem reared over his ledge like a cleaver above a chopping-block. He realised in panic that he was viewing it like a novice.

An old piton protruded from the bottom of the crack and he grabbed it for security while he steadied his swimming vision. It seemed to twitch like a rusty nail and he jerked his hand away with a yelp of fear.

He forced himself to concentrate on the sequence of footholds at the side of the crack. He had seconded it once before and been carefully briefed. There was a hidden hold over the top, he recalled, but was it right or left . . . or was that some other climb?

He dimly remembered a tense scrabble on the end of the rope

before a small handhold swung him out onto a grappling traverse. He looked in horror down the plunging cliff to the viciously impassive boulder-scree below. All the perspective of experience dissolved in his brain, and rock became an insuperable barrier again. But there *were* holds, he berated himself frantically. Holds! He had climbed much harder rock than this with ease. On a rope! He tried to imagine it around his waist, reassuringly taut in case of need.

He saw himself instead as something soft and wingless, trying to fly. His muscles slumped, helplessly.

A voice jeered from the horizontal past. "Twelve minutes." They were expecting him to slink sheepishly out of the gully.

Just another three minutes . . . he prayed in a pleading whisper. Three more minutes . . .

He clenched the side of the crack in a fierce grip, trembled his foot up onto a flat hold. It was still reversible.

Sweating fingertips grabbed a good edge inches higher. He stepped up again. Still reversible.

His body hung out from the crack, suspended from flimsy forearms. Fear locked his fingers like vice-grips on the holds. He tried to step down, dared not dislodge fingers or feet.

It was irreversible!

The roaring suction of the air clamped a kiss of death on his spider-life. Teeth ground in his head, his eyes screwed in agony as if the bone itself were clenching shut. Ankles shuttled and rattled, vibrating terror into the air. It was up . . . or off!

He kicked a toe higher in the groove, wrenched on his arms, shuddered up on the wedged foot, flung feeble fingers over the top of the crack . . . hurling a quenched flare of hope away. Fingers found a curved edge, rounded, smooth, slipping . . . He clung, his body an unbearable sack of lead, lurched his feet up again. Hidden friction lifted ounces off his arms.

Unlocking numbness, his fingers fled out of sight, scurrying desperately for the hidden hold. No feeling, but something hooked, held, hung. Hanging, he thrashed his right foot out and levered his weight up in agonised jerks. And the angle burst back, burst like the door of a car-crash slow-motion seconds before the fuel explodes. Threw him out onto the traverse.

He leaned in a groove above, gulping with dizzy nausea.

About to faint he fumbled for a handhold to anchor his body as waves of blackness ebbed and flowed. He was convulsed with the savagery of the struggle. Foul images seethed within him, over and over, his body hurtling out from the rock, wheeling and tumbling loose-limbed in the air, trailing a long, curling scarf of a scream. The bloody climax among the boulders repeated with the insistence of a jammed projector.

Behind the persuasive lie that was seducing him slowly into a swoon he felt the liquid throb of his blood-system. His body was a single pulse, a soft bag of shuddering blood jellying its way up the jagged granite.

He swayed out from the stance in a dizzy delirium, pulled himself back in again, pressing his chest against the cold, grey rock, nausea loosening his stomach and knotting his throat.

A tiny, bantering voice grew in his imagination: Do you want a rope Vinny a rope Vinny a rope . . .

A mean little playground tune.

He was mesmerised by the brutal texture of the mica-crusted rock sharpening and blurring in front of his eyes as his body swayed to the cyclic rhythm of the images falling and refalling in his mind. Minutes passed precariously as he balanced on the patient granite. Every harsh breath was a victory for survival.

He underwent a bitter, little death of the heart, and a slow unsteady regeneration.

Heroism, he learned, wasn't worth the fuss.

His legs were splayed apart across the groove, stiff and wooden as stilts. Every quiver of tension threatened to topple him. He began to move up slowly, controlling a hatred for the inorganic cruelty of rock.

Afterwards, he descended to base. There was no one there.

He collected his gear and went down through the boulders towards the track without a backward glance.

Mick was bellowing audible instructions to Janette from Aisling Arete. From the top of the crag they saw him diminish on the lakeside path to an incidental dot.

Vincent vanished from the club. He denied himself any curiosity about climbing, and never heard that he had started a crazy trend of time-trials.

A week later, a well-known climber soloed Prelude and Nightmare in five minutes.

Michael Bowler

THE LAST SEASON

I REMEMBER certain mornings between Spring and Summer,
After the long runs in the woods, after the Winter training,
when I experienced an extraordinary feeling of completion . . . an
exaltation. I burned with impatience to throw my strength into
the battles of the home straight. They would say to me: it's peak
form. I know now that it had another name – le bonheur. You
have never been truly young if you have not known such
moments. But one day the time comes when your best form will
never return and on rather a sad note you leave the games of
your youth forever. Yet you have achieved some fulfilment.
Sport teaches us to love life passionately and to accept it as it is
without cheating.

Michel Clare

When the evenings began to draw in I got that feeling. The dread
of darkness. Steeling my mind to face another winter's training.
Imagining relentless rains as I warmed up in the soft September
sun. I could feel the sweat oozing from my forehead as I flicked
my legs at the end of the warm up. The crispness wasn't there.

Michael Bowler was born in Cahirsiveen, County Kerry. He has spent
his working life as a Customs Officer in England. His main hobby is
athletics, and although basically a 10K runner, he has completed nine
marathons. His first novel, Destiny of Dreams, *was published in 1990*
and in 1993 he won the Irish Post/B&I Short Story competition.

The last race of a long season. I felt flat and adrenalin dry as I completed a few strides. Heavy legs and heavier heart.

The sharp crack of the starting gun made me pause. The 1500M field was away. I watched the initial burst down the back straight. The aristocrats of running. I felt a pang of nostalgia. It was once my event, in the seasons of my prime. When the speed was in my legs; I could change gear in a couple of strides.

I heard the timekeeper shout out the lap times 58, 59, 60 . . . I gave Simon a shout; we'd travelled up to the Palace together. He'd sent off the entries and talked me into a Ten K. It was an open meeting and the standard stretched like the field in the second lap. Four had broken away by the third lap with Simon tucked in at the leader's shoulder. He looked comfortable with that effortless bouncing style.

The sinking sun sliced through the four figures as they took the bell. The red vest Simon was wearing flamed for an instant, fusing with the fire in his face. I watched him closely as they came round knowing he didn't have a fast finish. I gave him another shout, seeing the suffering on the face of the leader. He seemed to incline his head, then he was off on an extended kick. The surprise move at 300 metres opened a short gap but the other three quickly recovered. I felt a slight surge of adrenalin for Simon as he hit the home straight. The gap squeezed as he began to tie up but he pumped his arms to carry his legs through the tape. The winner.

The next race was the Ten K and I jogged across to the start. Simon was just lifting his head; there was a glazed look in his eyes. I knew the feeling well: the whirling head, the rapid rasp in the throat and the lactic in the legs. But, the flying feeling as you kicked for home was worth all the puny pain at the end. I said "Great run, Simon," as I sat down to put on my spikes. Simon found his legs before he found his voice.

"Thanks Kieran. It was bloody hard work."

I laughed lightly. "I know, knew rather."

Simon smiled. "Go on, you've still got it, old boy."

I got up, laughing, and he called after me, "Have a good one."

I had time for three strides before the red coated starter called us to the line. It was a big field and I found a place well away from the inside lane. On your marks . . . the gun raised the runners from their crouches. Meditation in motion. After a desperate lunge for the bend the field settled down to a relaxed rhythm. I dropped off the pace and switched off. Steady state running for 25 laps. Concentration became crucial as the laps peeled away. I tried not to notice the lap markers as we came round each time. Years of conditioning made me divide the distance into miles. Feeling free and fluid after a mile. Digging in at two miles as the pace quickened. Surge upon surge down the back straight with the slight breeze. The field finally falling away in total disintegration.

At Five K that sinking feeling that you had to do it all again. Only twice as hard. Running into oxygen debt, your legs going lazy with lactic. The purifying pain that raises the runner above automatons. Christ! The bloody agony! Another burst down the back straight. The leader trying to break away. Stay with it. My lungs labouring. Legs dying under me. I could feel the stinging sweat rolling down my cheeks like bitter tears. A haze before my eyes as we finish another lap. Was that eight? Can't go through it again! The pain barrier is the figment of a masochist imagination. Must be six? I wiped away the sweat with the back of my right hand. Another miserable mile. Then a lousy lap . . . and . . . the bell. Another savage surge. The remainder of the field cracks. Only three through the figment; the trailing pack pale fragments in the setting sun. Going down . . . gold, silver and bronze. Cold concentration on the two front runners.

Every metre mattered now. The pace seemed to settle into a tactical tempo. Waiting for the last lap. I forged to the front on the home straight. Token try. The bell . . . The catalyst setting up the supreme sacrifice. Like a pageant of pain the three runners carried the colours and cross of the crowd. Sharing pride and pain 300 metres from calvary. Shadows shortening around the arena. A freshening breeze across the brow. I held the lead at 200 metres, feeling a fleeting elation. They were on my shoulder. Poised . . . I couldn't lift my knees as they pushed past, engaged in their own private battle. Off the last bend . . . they were gone, into gold and silver. I tried again down the home straight. Leaden legs driven by iron will. It wasn't there. Either the legs or the will had wilted. The finishing line. Home. Calvary conquered. Leaning over the steeplechase barrier. Feeling sick, faint, sad. The tragic trinity. Someone put a palm in my hand.

"Well run."

Palm. Peace. I shook the hand weakly. The winners.

My legs wobbled when I tried to walk again. The sweat was cold in the small of my back. Simon came over and handed me my tracksuit.

"You really took them on in the last lap, Kieran."

"Well to tell the truth I was tying up at the bell," I admitted.

"Your reserves must be well in the black then."

We were interrupted by the results being announced. Name and time flashed onto the giant scoreboard. Bright bronze. Fading light flung from the imminent night sky.

Simon warmed down with me even though he'd already jogged a mile. I felt the lactic lighten in my legs as we finished. A quick shower and we were on the road. I relaxed while Simon took the wheel. Talking of training and times. Mileage and memories.

He was bound for Israel in October. The simple socialist alternative to the American scholarship system. It was a letter in

Runners Review inviting athletes to Israel that prompted him. To work six hours a day in a kibbutz and to train in the sunlit citrus groves. Imagine. Idyllic days in December working on the land, holy land, lapped by the Sea of Galilee. Soft breezes from the hills fanning your face as you ran. In the evening of my athletic life. One more Everest to climb. The marathon. The mountain in my mind. When I read the international fixture list in the *Review* the dream began. "The outstanding event of the Israeli athletic calendar is the Sea of Galilee International Marathon around the holy and historic lake on December 20th!" I realized Israel wasn't alien; outside of Ireland it was the first land in my living memory.

Was not Jerusalem the city state I was searching for in the agony of exile. The ephemeral Peace I almost touched in my twenties. In the long walks through a little Kerry town. Enclosed in a verdant valley. The Summer sun laid to rest. A scattered reflection in the river. Shadows fading from the hills. Across the lonely road where my father was killed. A silence falling over the night.

It was past midnight when we got home both tired and troubled with our own thoughts. On the second Saturday in October Simon flew to Tel Aviv. We went for a pint with a few of the middle distance squad before he left. I felt a certain sadness as we said goodbye to my training partner. Although it was six years since the Yom Kippur war the Middle East was still ravelled in a colonial contradiction.

In November I began the twenty mile runs every Sunday morning. The first ten miles through the little village of Wakering were relaxed, my breath condensed in the crisp air . . . at fifteen the tingling in the thighs as the distance told. The last five miles with legs like lead; dead to the world for the rest of the day. Slumped in front of the telly watching the Big Match and drinking litres of orange juice.

Staying in every weekend; waiting for a letter from Simon.
Taking my running gear to the launderette on Friday night.
Shopping for the week on Saturday. Sometimes feeling restless
and lonely in the weekend shopping crowd. Out of this mood I
began to dabble in writing. During my Wednesday ten I got the
feeling for the first vignette. It was a skinning cold night; I
pushed the pace from the beginning to get warm. After five miles
my mind was floating halfway between Bethlehem and Beentee,
a hill of home. I stole a Christmas scene from my childhood.
Buried deep to build a personal pyre to my father. A reflection
of his light. A guilt offering that I didn't believe in his everlasting
life.

One Saturday I ran into Yussuf in the library. He was a history
teacher I used to share digs with when I first arrived in this town.
I had picked out four books on the Middle East. Over a cup of
coffee in the cafe I told him I was thinking of going to Israel for
a race.

"Kieran my friend, Israel is a reality even for an Arab
historian. Go by all means with your eyes and mind open.
You're ready to suffer for your race. But think as you run: is
your agony anything compared to the pain of the Palestinians?"

I didn't respond for a moment. I drained my coffee cup.

"Of course I'll try to understand, Yussuf."

"Palestine is people as well as land. Subject to suffering
without a home, scarcely a hope."

"But Yussuf, you dreamed yourself free in Egypt. You once
told me that instead of being a teacher you could have been
tending a flock on the banks of the Nile."

"Personally I think it would be more meaningful than teaching
history to ignorant amnesiacs!"

"Seriously, I believe the Palestinians will have a State someday
and in the meantime I feel that I can learn more by travelling."

"*Asalaam aleikum*, Kieran, Peace be upon thee." Yussuf gave his blessing on my journey. As we parted I said I'd send him a card from "Palestine" and he laughed and shook my hand.

After an early afternoon five miles I settled down to read. Green March, Black September; the story of the Palestinian Arabs. I became so engrossed in the tragic story that I missed Man United on "Match of the Day". The longing in their Literature, the pain in their poetry . . .

> Write down,
> I am an Arab
> I am a name without a title,
> Steadfast in a frenzied world
> My roots sink deep
> Beyond the ages,
> Beyond time.

I lay awake a long time; the night turned and my mind found succour in sleep.

Next morning I started my last long run in a grey mist. Going through the first ten miles in 65 minutes with a cold wind against me. I tried to keep the rhythm going along the seafront, the wind wild in my hair. I vowed to visit the barber as a gust nearly took me off my feet. The last three miles dragged and the little incline on the Boulevard became as hard as a hill. Once I cleared the last summit my mind had drifted to the shores of Galilee.

The elation of the run lingered into Monday. A weak winter sun glinted on the grass in Priory Park. A green prism through a film of frost. I seemed to flow over a forest. My mind cleared away the offal of the office. The naked trees trembling in a shadow. A cooling cloud across my wet brow. Into the sun for the second lap. Frozen faces filing from a tower block. Turning collars and noses up. I float across their path; beyond the life of concrete creatures. The grass softens under my feet and I find myself in its silence. I faintly hear my breathing, feel my footsteps. My mind and my body are suspended. One. Time better spent, in pubs and clubs. Disco here and disco there. Disco nowhere. The moment when running is simply a sacrifice. As close to the sacred silence of the soul as I could ever get.

After that five miles in the forest of my dreams the week was denuded of daylight. By Saturday I could write 100 miles for the week in my diary and my mind was ready for the marathon.

Christmas crowds rushed in and out of shops. Tarnished tinsel on a Christmas tree growing out of the hardness of the High Street. I got caught up in the mercenary madness as I bought an instamatic in Boots. As I was buffeted by the hordes I wondered would there be peace on the West Bank, in Bethlehem.

My last day in the office was interminable. The afternoon dragged; a dreary mist fell across the window. Passing time over a tea cup. Later packing my travelling bag with tee shirts and jeans. The night before flying out I was going to spend at Aunt Aine's in London. The mist had multiplied when I finally caught the train at five.

Snatches of Christmas conversation on the Underground. Glossy ads glorifying plastic people. I read the meaningless messages to avoid the insolent eyes of a scut of skinheads. The rain had ceased when I reached Muswell Hill. The night was quiet, the streets bleak. Only one old man shuffled past me as I walked to my aunt's. He held a carrier bag in one hand. He was looking in doorways, searching for a home. So this was the streets of London. The last loneliness. The longest. Aunt Aine had kept a dinner for me but I could only pick at it. I felt tired and ventured to bed at ten. I lay awake listening to the late night trains. The endless journeying.

I travelled in a dream during the night, a sadness shrouding my subconscious. I witnessed myself in stone silence staring for the last time through the front window at home. Rainclouds ebbing away the restless evening. The hills huddled on the horizon, defining darkness. The rain comes pelting down.

I look at the clock on the mantelpiece; the one made in China. The time is twenty past nine. There is no knowing whether it is morning or night. But I'm leaving. My mother's face is drenched with tears. I reach out but can't find her hand. I board the morning bus. Passing through the soft shadow of the hills and into the nowhere of neon.

Another morning. Sounds seeping into my room. A child's voice; inarticulate tears. A train catching the echo of a tremor at the bedroom window. I drew the curtains across the day. Rain faded light found the time on my watch.

I left in good time for Heathrow. I had to be there by midday although the flight wasn't until two o'clock. Israeli security had me opening my carefully packed bag. They didn't quite understand my pronunciation of Kibbutz Ginossar as I explained the reason for my trip. My Hebrew was hairy. I ended up discussing the merits of my Nike Elite racers with one of them who did a bit of running. After moping around the concourse the flight was finally called. I found a seat on the last coach across the tarmac.

I glanced once more at the grey sky and couldn't wait to leave London. Within ten minutes we were in the air. *El Al:* To the skies.

Acknowledgements

Michael Bowler: *The Last Season,* © Michael Bowler 1994, reprinted by permission of the author. Daniel Corkery: *The Lartys,* © Executors of Daniel Corkery, reprinted by permission of The Educational Company of Ireland. Christine Dwyer-Hickey: *Across the Excellent Grass,* © Christine Dwyer-Hickey 1992, reprinted by permission of the author. Brian Friel: *The Widowhood System,* © Brian Friel 1979, reprinted by permission of Curtis Brown, London. John B. Keane: *"You're On Next Sunday",* © John B. Keane 1976, reprinted by permission of the author. Bryan MacMahon: *My Love Has a Long Tail,* © Bryan MacMahon 1985, reprinted by permission of A.P. Watt Ltd., on behalf of the author. Sam McAughtry: *Play Up and Play the Game,* © Sam McAughtry 1994, reprinted by permission of the author. Patrick Moran: *Almost All-Ireland,* © Patrick Moran 1984, reprinted by permission of the author. Mary Morrissy: *The Butterfly,* © Mary Morrissy 1985, reprinted by permission of the author. Seán O'Faoláin: *The End of a Good Man,* from *Teresa and Other Stories* (Jonathan Cape), © the Estate of Seán O'Faoláin, reprinted by permission of Rogers, Coleridge & White Ltd. Liam O'Flaherty: *The Wing Three-Quarter* from *The Short Stories of Liam O'Flaherty* (Jonathan Cape), reprinted by permission of the Peters, Fraser & Dunlop Group Ltd. T.P. O'Mahony: *The Bowlplayer,* © T.P. O'Mahony 1971, reprinted by permission of the author. Dermot Somers: *Cliff Hanger,* © Dermot Somers 1984. Reprinted by permission of the author. Somerville and Ross: *The Policy of the Closed Door,* © Edith Oenone Somerville and Martin Ross, reprinted by permission of Curtis Brown Group Ltd., London. Padraic Ó Conaire: *The Trout in the Big River*, translation © David Marcus. Every effort has been made to obtain permission from the copyright holders. The publishers would be glad to hear from any copyright holders not acknowledged.